"With a vulnerable and generous heart, Robert Lesoine shares the mindsets and heart-sets that contribute to healing in the aftermath of a loved one's suicide. Written in compassionate and practical language, this book invites you into a journey of restoration, reminding you that you can still laugh, love, and come full circle with your departed loved one."
—Reverend Michael Bernard Beckwith, Founder and Spiritual Director, Agape International Spiritual Center, author of *Spiritual Liberation*

"Suicide is a pain that never quite disappears. This eloquent book is a personal companion for those left behind, a friend nudging us forward with compassion and wisdom to see below, behind, and beyond the limitations of our current understanding. Highly recommended for anyone who wishes to keep the heart open after losing a loved one in this way."
—Christopher Germer, PhD, Clinical Instructor, Harvard Medical School, author of *The Mindful Path to Self-Compassion*

"An extraordinary piece of work. This book is tough to read and impossible to put down. Recovering from a loved one's suicide requires nothing less than everything we have. We need courage and real tools to approach the wounded heart unflinchingly, with love and wisdom. Marilynne Chöphel and Robert Lesoine provide those real tools, abundantly. It is possible to start again. Reading *Unfinished Conversation* will prove that over and over."
—Richard Heckler PhD, author of *Waking Up, Alive*

"Thank you for the courage to look into this well of darkness and despair plaguing modernity and the world as a whole. More importantly, thank you for your courage to excavate the tragic and for making it yield the healing gems hidden within. May this gift serve as a map and a guide to numberless people trapped in this dark landscape of sorrow, and longing to come home."
—Malidoma Patrice Somé, author of *Ritual* and *The Healing Wisdom of Africa*

"A welcome interdisciplinary resource for addressing the devastating impacts of suicide that facilitates the all-important healing process of grieving."

—Joseph Bobrow, PhD, Founder, The Coming Home Project,
providing support for Iraq and Afghanistan veterans,
service members, and their families

"A wise, deep, and powerful book... pulsing with honesty... it offers a path through suffering to some resolution and understanding. The authors handle a difficult topic with Grace."

—Fred Luskin PhD, Director, Stanford Forgiveness Project,
author of *The Nine Steps to Forgiveness*

"A comprehensive toolbox for managing the sudden, violent loss that is suicide. We need all the help we can get to stay sane in the face of suffering."

—Marilyn Pittman, actor, radio host. Creator of the award-winning
2011 Off-Broadway production "It's All The Rage"

"This is exactly the kind of book I was looking for when I experienced the heart-wrenching loss of my daughter to suicide fifteen years ago. Robert shares his personal journey through grief with a profound and anguished honesty. *Unfinished Conversation* offers hope for healing and the possibility that great suffering can be transformed. I recommend this thoughtful and heartfelt book to other survivors searching for a way through the dark valley of grief."

—Nancy Coughlan, Bereaved Parents Support Group Facilitator

Unfinished Conversation

UNFINISHED CONVERSATION

Healing from Suicide and Loss

A GUIDED JOURNEY

Robert E. Lesoine

with Marilynne Chöphel, MFT

PARALLAX
PRESS

Berkeley, California

Parallax Press
P.O. Box 7355
Berkeley, California 94707
www.parallax.org

Parallax Press is the publishing division of Unified Buddhist Church, Inc.
© 2013 by Robert E Lesoine and Marilynne Chöphel
All rights reserved
Printed in the United States of America

Cover collage by Gopa & Ted2 from images from istockphoto and Thinkstock.
Back cover photo of Robert E. Lesoine © Spencer Lowell;
photo of Marilynne Chöphel © Curtis Grindahle
Cover and text design by Gopa & Ted2, Inc.

Library of Congress Cataloging-in-Publication Data
is available upon request.

1 2 3 4 5 / 17 16 15 14 13

This book is dedicated to all survivors.

May your unbearable loss

give rise to great compassion and courageous love.

TABLE OF CONTENTS

APPENDICES

PREFACE

UNFINISHED CONVERSATION invites us to take a journey directly into the pain of our loss. This may be a journey we are reluctant to go on. After what we've already been through, to remember again, to awaken our lost loved one inside us, can feel like opening wounds. Yet the saying is true: The way out is *through*. As we walk through the feelings and memories we've been left with by the suicide, facing rather than fearing them, allowing rather than holding back, shining light into the darkness, we find our way out of the wrenching grief of our loss. This book skillfully guides us on that journey.

There is no loss quite like having a loved one take his or her own life. Our hearts are ripped open by knowing that those we cared about were in a darkness and despair so deep that they violently turned against themselves. We may want to shut down, withdraw, perhaps hide from others what happened. We may have trouble sleeping as we lie awake reviewing over and over again the circumstances of the suicide. Scarcely an hour may pass without tragic memories of our loved one arising in our mind. The days and hours leading up to their end may haunt us as we, like skilled prosecutors, question ourselves to see what we might have done differently. Their end is tragic and final, and now we belong to a club we never wanted to be in—we are survivors.

Some say we never get over the suicide of a loved one. We certainly never forget it, but we can heal our shattered hearts and even develop a new relationship with the one who is now gone. In *Unfinished Conversation*, Robert and Marilynne offer us the opportunity to do just that. Robert opens his own journal to reveal how, after the death of his closest friend, he was able to move over time from raw pain, sorrow, and anger to deeper love and forgiveness of both his friend and himself.

We may come to this book with our own unique stories of lost parents, husbands and wives, sisters and brothers, children, teachers, friends, and coworkers. The details of our stories may be very different from Robert's, but the process of grieving is the same. We walk through the same dark corridors toward the light of healing. Robert and Marilynne expertly and compassionately guide us in creating our own journals, knowing that as we remember our loved ones, as we delve into and explore their lives and ours, as we talk to and with them, we write our way into and out of our deep grief. Whether we lost our loved one recently or years ago, this journey can bring back to us the parts of ourselves that were also lost and join them again in wholeness.

I first read Robert's story nearly twenty-five years after my sister Carol took her life. Writing and crying my way through the questions and suggestions wove a new and profound element into my ongoing healing. I picked up the unfinished conversation with my sister where it had left off. I joined a support group with other survivors. I could finally say the word "sister" without wobbling. Her suicide was no longer always the first thing on my mind on waking, nor did thoughts of her and her end continually intrude upon the hours of my days. I felt returned to life, not diminished by the loss but strengthened by the healing.

One of my favorite metaphors for profound healing comes from the traditional Japanese tea ceremony. Special pottery bowls are used in this ritual of communion. If a tea bowl breaks, its pieces are joined together again with gold. These mended bowls are considered to be the most valuable and prized, because they've been broken and made whole again. Remembering, reflecting, forgiving, and loving is the gold that mends our brokenness. It isn't an easy path to healing, but it's a sure one.

As we read these chapters and write in our own journals, as we open the door and the pain of memories and feelings rush out to meet us, it's important to remember that we're here now in this present moment. We're not back there, trapped in the horror. We're breathing this air, sitting on this floor, looking around this room. The feelings of the past may be alive in us, but the circumstances of our lives are different now. We are connected to this present; we have this tool to guide us; we can reach out for support. As Marilynne puts it, we do this work of remembering in order to heal, not to retraumatize. By keeping one foot in the present as we enter the past, we're able to be *with* the trauma, not *in* the trauma.

This is what the journal writing does. It keeps us conscious in the present moment even as we relate to the past. As we allow ourselves to write without judgment and without editing, freely allowing ourselves to catch the thread of the stories stuck inside us, the natural creativity of the mind begins to reshape them, reveal what is beneath, and loosen their control over our lives. Writing moves the energy. As we shine the light of consciousness on the past, we are led into the present, which is exactly where we want to be. Now, not then.

This process works . . . if we do it. We have to write the pain and by doing so, release it. As Robert discovered, journaling allows us to heal ourselves from within. We clarify our thoughts and feelings in the privacy and safety of our own journals, and there we also meet our loved one who is still alive inside us. We can take this journey on our own or with a friend, ideally another survivor. Using *Unfinished Conversation* as the guiding structure for a support group can bring profound healing in communion with others. To sit with a group of survivors is an invitation to meet a courage and an authenticity we don't often find in daily life.

After my own experience of reading and following the suggestions in this book, I felt called to offer this method in a support group. We meet every other week, open and raw together. It's not easy. We'd all rather go to a movie or do anything else but sit there facing the truth of what seems incomprehensible. But as one participant said, "We never want to come here, but then once we start talking with each other, we don't want to stop." Moving through the pain and sorrow and anger together with other survivors opens our hearts in love and compassion. At the end of each meeting, we stand in a circle and look around to meet the loving eyes of those we're traveling with on this journey. When we bend to blow out the candles we've each lit for our loved ones, and then turn back into our own worlds, we do so knowing that we're held in the shared framework of *Unfinished Conversation*. We know that the others in the group are meeting themselves and their loved ones along the same route.

Whether we walk this path alone or with others, as we give ourselves the gift of healing in this way, we can come to define our loved ones not by how they died but by how they lived. We can be healed into a heart no longer broken but opened in compassion. And we ourselves can choose to live more fully, not in spite of their death but because of it.

Shoshana Alexander
Coauthor, with James Baraz, of
Awakening Joy: 10 Steps to Happiness
April 2013

Unfinished Conversation

Our fifteen-year conversation was about life and love,
poetry and politics, women, sex, and baseball.

Our conversation was about letting wisdom and compassion
express through each of us. Our conversation was about
beauty and light and creativity.

Our conversation was about saying "Yes" to life and to the
passion of being alive . . . . Now there is only silence.

~ Robert Lesoine

1: The Journey Begins

I AM SITTING in the dentist's chair when my cell phone rings. All I hear is screaming and crying. I can't make out who is calling or what the person is saying. Finally, I hear the person yell, "Larry has killed himself!" I realize it's Mary, Larry's ex-wife.

Larry Harpel is my closest friend so I know there must be some mistake. In my mind I shout, *This is all wrong. This can't be happening.* But I can only sit in helpless shock with my mouth full of dental equipment and cotton swabs, while the hygienist completes the procedure. A heavy ache begins to grow in the pit of my stomach.

When I leave, I call Mary back. She is mostly incoherent, but manages to give me the number of the coroner's office. She thinks they will want us to identify the body. *Maybe it's not him?*

I hang up, and, with clammy, trembling hands and constricted throat, I punch in the numbers on my cell phone. My call is answered by a strangely upbeat coroner's attendant. He confirms that Lawrence Harpel's body is at the morgue and has already been identified by his driver's license. There is no need for us to view the body.

Larry Harpel took his life on the night of October 15, 2005. The other victims of this tragedy are the survivors of his suicide—his loved ones and friends. Those of us who lose someone to suicide are left to come to terms with the trauma we experience when a loved one chooses "self-slaughter," as Shakespeare called it. The death of anyone we love is hard enough to accept, but when it is a suicide, we are left facing a cold, blank wall, without solace or comprehension. And even as we search for a meaning, at first it may elude us. I stood at that wall myself, torn between wanting to punch it in rage and longing to simply dissolve into oblivion. It was my search for understanding, healing, and forgiveness that motivated me to begin writing to Larry. I deliberately set out to finish my conversation with him through an ongoing journal that became the basis of this book.

All suicides are unfinished conversations. There is so much that we, the living, still need to say and want to hear from those who take their own lives, leaving us with no opportunity to communicate. But there are ways that writing can be used as a means of continuing the conversation between the departed and the survivor. I don't mean this in any supernatural sense; I mean simply putting pen to paper.

While you may want to talk about the exercises with someone you trust, or simply reflect on them, I would encourage you to actually write your thoughts and feelings in your own Grief and Healing Journal. For it is in these private pages that a person begins to reestablish the revived conversation with the departed. It is in those personal moments, and only there, that the conversation can unfold, and with it the eventual healing that the writer of the journal will experience as I did. I strongly believe that this process of self-healing really comes from writing it down—or the struggle to write it down. This is as simple as writing a letter over and over again. We can all do it. You don't have to be a "writer" to do it. Trust it as a method, as a tool through grief to wholeness.

You might start by choosing an exercise you feel ready to respond to, then returning to the others later when and if it feels right. Journaling your experience will allow you to say all that you may have wanted to say when your loved one was alive, or to reveal your reactions to what he or she has done. This is an opportunity to express your emotions—all of your regret, all of your anger and disappointment, and perhaps, all of your understanding and love.

You may think it's better to avoid painful emotions, but that avoidance will simply bury them. I was not even aware of all the anger and betrayal I felt until I began to express these feelings in writing. So I learned that by turning toward the pain, at a pace that was manageable, I could find my way through it. The responses to loss are unique to each person, and all are quite normal reactions to an event as life altering as losing someone you love to suicide. Any unresolved grief or trauma from the past also compounds the complexity of your current loss. Distressing symptoms remain trapped in the mind and body, easily triggered by everyday reminders of the trauma—sometimes for months or years— unless resolved in some way. You can't change what happened in the past, but you can transform the mind's and the body's responses to the past. Only by facing and befriending your complicated feelings, with honesty and compassion, can you truly heal and reclaim your life after such loss. (See Appendix 1, "Tool Kit for Your Journey to Healing" and Appendix 2, "Creating Support" for suggestions on important ways to give yourself support during this time.)

Write as if your loved one is in front of you, hearing everything you are saying. *Make it real.* The most important part of what you will be doing is having an honest conversation, the one you didn't have a chance to finish. Whatever helps you to have this conversation, whether it's more emotion or coming from a place of calm, will be valuable.

Some of your writing may even take the form of interactive dialogues between you and your loved one. Write what you have to say, then listen for a response and write it, whatever it is. You will find it easier than you think to capture the voice of the person you lost. Try it. The benefit that you will gain in finishing your particular conversation will go far beyond what you can imagine.

Healing and grieving take time. So make a personal commitment to continue this process for as long as it takes. Keep the communication between you and the departed open until you have expressed whatever has been bottled up inside since the suicide, whether that was days, months, or even years ago. I suggest that you continue your writing process until you attain some sense of clarity, release, and resolution.

In the beginning I recommend that you choose a specific length of time to commit to writing on a regular basis. Initially, I wrote each day for forty-nine days following my friend's death. I chose this length of time for my written mourning because in Buddhism, which is my particular spiritual practice, the forty-nine-day period after death is considered the time during which the consciousness of the departed is suspended between one incarnation and the next. Other religions also have traditions that call for a period of time to grieve and honor the deceased. In Judaism there's a seven-day period of mourning after death known as "sitting shiva," followed by a year of prayer and healing that ends with the placing of a headstone and a second memorial service. For some Christians, "the wake" is a vigil with the body of the deceased, and in many cultures black clothing or a black armband is worn for a full year after the death as a sign of mourning.

Think of the time you dedicate to your bereavement as holding a vigil or sitting shiva over "the body of your grief." Whatever length of time you choose, I recommend that you commit to daily writing and other forms of self-expression, to give your mourning period a shape and structure to support and facilitate your healing process.

After completing my initial period of journaling, I found myself still writing, because there was much that had been left unspoken. Be open to the realizations and insights that may continue to arise. For so great a loss, a certain level of grief may be with you for the rest of your life. But if you truly mourn, if you truly feel and express the deep grief that comes from a sudden loss by suicide of a loved one, in time you will feel whole again. Completing your unfinished conversation will be an important key to this healing. (See Appendix 3, "Clinical Theory Behind *Unifinished Conversations*'s Healing Process.)

As you embark on your journey, remember to stay in the light of your grief. However you experience it—be it rage, unbearable sorrow, or the agonizing angst of regret—your ongoing grieving process will allow you to access the pathways that lead you to forgiveness, acceptance, and peace. In time, your grief can begin to illuminate the truths that you know and live for. This book is offered to you in the hope that your grieving and healing journey may bring you a renewed relationship with yourself, your life, and with your loved one.

The Journey Begins
Journal Exercises

BEGINNING YOUR JOURNAL

FIRST REACTIONS

ABOUT THE TOOL KIT FOR YOUR JOURNEY TO HEALING

: This is where your journey begins. Choose a notebook to use as your Grief and Healing Journal and keep it nearby. For your first entry, allow your loved one to come into your awareness, and imagine him or her standing before you. Notice the feelings, thoughts, and physical sensations that arise inside. Take a few deep breaths and when you're ready, write some words, phrases, or sentences to describe what you're noticing within yourself.

> Example: "As I think about losing him, I feel a gripping in my stomach and a knot in my throat. Currents of anxiety surge through me with each thought. I feel a heavy sinking feeling of deep, deep sadness. My thoughts are racing and my mind feels in a fog . . ."

: The moment when you first become aware of your loved one's death is perhaps the most devastating. It is important to approach those memories slowly, with honor and great care, and relate with them in manageable increments. Remember to stay in the here-and-now as you reflect on the past. Take your time. When you're ready to remember your feelings and the events of that moment, gently observe your reactions, and write them in your journal. Using the present tense can help you to access your experience more fully.

: Where are you and how do you first become aware that your loved one has taken his or her own life? Example: "I am sitting in the dentist's chair when . . ."

: What are your first reactions? Notice the emotions, thoughts, and experiences in your body in those first moments. What do you do—or not do?

: Now observe the emotions and physical sensations inside yourself right now, in this present moment. Write about the qualities you would like to bring forward to meet these painful feelings, such as understanding, sensitivity, kindness, empathy, perspective, compassion.

: Appendix 1, "Tool Kit for Your Journey to Healing" offers many suggestions for ways to take care of yourself during this time of healing, like meeting your experience with nonjudgment and compassion, sharing your experience with others who truly understand and care, and choosing activities that help you feel safe, comforted, and connected with yourself and others. Look over the Tool Kit, and then in your journal make a list of your Inner and Outer Resources and ways in which you can care for yourself as you grieve and heal.

Returning to the present moment . . .

Bring awareness into your body, soften your belly,
and allow full gentle breaths. With each exhalation,
allow your body to soften and relax.

I am present in this moment,
relaxing and breathing.

2: SHOCK AND DISBELIEF

I HANG UP deeply shaken after talking to the coroner. In a fog I walk to my car, sit silently at the wheel for a few minutes, and, after some deep breaths, pick up my cell phone and begin to contact the others.

Larry and I were cofounders of a men's support group called The Lost and Found Men's Council. For the past fifteen years a small group of us had met every two weeks. We had no specific program except to foster communication and brotherhood. We drummed, lit ritual candles, invoked sacred space, and shared our lives with one another. Each summer we went on a weekend camping retreat that provided a time for creating our own healing practices and a chance for deeper communication. We tapped into the council fire traditions of Native American, African, and other indigenous cultures where for time immemorial men have sat together talking, listening, and sharing with one another. We drew upon ritual, poetry, and myth to support each member's self-realization, and we continue to do so, now without Larry. The brothers of the Lost and Found all considered him to be the heart and soul of our men's council.

I call "brother" Bruce and catch him on his way to an appointment with his therapist. He's driving on the 405 Freeway in Los Angeles, where we all live. My voice quavers as I hear myself speak the words out loud for the first time. Bruce is stunned. He tells me that he has just hung up from leaving a message on Larry's voice mail. We lose the phone connection in the middle of our conversation. While waiting for him to call back, I call Jeff, who works as a sound editor at Universal Studios. Jeff gets it immediately.

When Bruce finally reaches me again, he says he had to pull over on to the shoulder of the jammed freeway to try to comprehend what I'd just said. He's in suspicious disbelief. "This is no joke," I tell him. "Listen to me. Larry has killed himself. It's not a mistake. I wish it were. I just spoke to a guy at the morgue. His body's already been identified."

I don't phone Cory until I get home. He's out working late on a DVD project, so I leave a voice mail. Later he too tells me he thought it was just a prank. He'd phoned Larry immediately and left a message asking if it was a joke. There was no reply.

Later I make a call to brother Ken, an acupuncturist, but unable to reach him, I just say it's an urgent call. At 6:30 a.m. the next morning, Ken phones, thinking I need an emergency appointment. There's silence on the line after I break it to him.

That evening I begin to scribble my first reactions in my journal. *What a messed up thing to do, Larry man. I want to slap some sense into that thick bald head of his. Larry, that was a rotten, cowardly, selfish thing for you to do. You copped out. You've had the last word and it is a pitiful useless word! You were not the man I thought you were.*

Larry, you let the bastards beat you! I am so sorry. I love you so much, but you betrayed that love. I am so angry at you that I can't grieve. It was a bad idea, Larry! You ran away from us.

I keep on seeing the lonesome eyes of your beautiful big bear of a dog— Buddy. How could you do this to him*? How could you leave him . . . and us like this? I thought you were a man of courage. I was wrong. I am so sad that it has come to this.*

We shared such a deep friendship for so many years that your death is a crushing blow. I know that eventually I will miss you terribly. But not yet! I am so furious that I just can't get my head around what you did. I do not excuse or accept your act. I can't help but see it as cowardice, my brother, and I will hold you accountable. I want to grieve, but tonight I have no tears.

Shock and Disbelief
Journal Exercises

TELLING OTHERS

THE FIRST DAY

BEGINNING THE CONVERSATION

: When you found out that your loved one had died, who were the first people you contacted? What were their reactions? What were your reactions to their reactions?

: What happened during those first twenty-four hours? Create a chronology of events noting your changing thoughts, physical sensations, and feelings as you went through that first day. What did you and others do—or not do?

: Begin your first "conversation" with your loved one. The easiest way to do this is to put it in the form of a letter, beginning with his or her name. Then just write. What did you want to say to him immediately after you found out he was gone? What do you want to say right now?

Example:
Dear Larry,
I'm writing to you because it is the only way I can speak to you anymore.
It is only twenty-four hours since I learned that you took your own life
and I can't get used to you not being around. I also can't really accept that
you left me the way you did . . .

Returning to the present moment . . .

As you sit comfortably, feel where your body makes contact with
the chair or the floor beneath you. When you breathe in, relax your
body and lengthen your spine. When you breathe out, let
your body be held by the support beneath you.

I am grounded and supported in the present.

3: DISREGARDED WARNINGS

NINE DAYS BEFORE his suicide Larry had hosted the Lost and Found men's group in his small two-room apartment in Venice, California. That night's meeting followed our usual structure. We began with a period of free-form drumming, listening to each man's voice speak through his drum. We "called in" the seven directions of Native American tradition, and asked the grandfathers and ancestral guides to bless and join with us in council. We lit a stick of sage and "smudged," bathing each man in the sacred smoke to clear his energy and to purify our meeting space.

Then each of us lit a candle and placed it on our ritual log, which is covered with the residue of fifteen years of wax drippings from past meetings. We each took a turn holding the "talking stick" and speaking our mind. After each speaker, there was a brief period of feedback or, as we call it, "cross talk."

That night as Larry held the talking stick, I remember him expressing feelings of self-doubt and low self-esteem, as he had for the past few meetings. In September, just a month before his suicide, he had begun a new job teaching a fourth-grade class at a school in Pacific Palisades. It was his first return to the classroom after four years, due to a debilitating arm injury. While Larry loved teaching poetry and language arts, he was now feeling underqualified to teach the math and science curriculum. Yet, he told us, he had been going into class *cold* each morning without being adequately prepared or planning his lessons. He lamented, "Some days are good. Some are just awful."

I commented that maybe it was a bad idea to wing it like that. He told us he was just too tired and unmotivated to plan. We all reminded him of his past successes as a teacher and strongly "suggested" that he buckle down and get with the program. And we all gave him lots of support. He was resistant.

Besides feeling such low self-esteem, just a few weeks prior Larry had reinjured his arm while playing softball and was experiencing constant pain from his shoulder down to his wrist. He couldn't find relief, and he hadn't been sleeping well. One of the worst parts was that the pain brought back the memory of an earlier arm injury he'd experienced four years before which had left him incapacitated. Unable to work, he'd been forced to live off a small disability check while he waited for the verdict in an insurance lawsuit that had dragged on year after year.

The last thing I remember Larry saying during his check-in that evening was that recently his arm pain had been so bad that if he'd had a gun he would have ended it all. "I can't go through unrelenting pain like that again," he told us. He had alluded to suicide before on the rare occasion, but none of us had taken him seriously. We didn't this time either. I realize now that it was a grave mistake.

Only after Larry's death did I learn that early warnings of suicidal ideation should always be taken seriously, and we should refer anyone having suicidal thoughts to a qualified mental health professional or to a suicide hotline. Looking back, I now recognize the signs of Larry's potential suicide—his loss of purpose and meaning, anxiety and agitation, feeling hopeless and worthless, despair, uncontrolled anger and frustration, sleeplessness, and wanting to give up. Nothing that I or anyone else was saying seemed to get through the thick veil of his self-doubt.

A few days after that men's meeting, Bruce and I went over to Larry's to watch the Angels beat the White Sox on TV. Bruce, a White Sox fan, wasn't happy. Larry, a dedicated lifetime follower of the Boston Red Sox, was uncharacteristically neutral. He was usually crazy about baseball, but that night he was down and extremely negative. He continued to talk about his feelings of self-doubt and that he just didn't want to grade his students' papers. I suggested that he let the students assess and grade themselves. He wasn't interested. It seemed to me that part of him wanted to teach but another part didn't want to do what was required. I told him this sounded like laziness. He didn't want to hear that either.

When he complained about the constant pain in his arm, I suggested that he consider giving up playing softball. "Oh, thanks a lot, Bob!" he said angrily, "You want me to give up the one thing that really brings me joy. Well, forget about it, man! If I couldn't ever play ball again, my life wouldn't be worth living."

"It was just a suggestion, my brother. But do whatever the hell you want," I replied, throwing my hands up in resignation. That night was the last time I saw Larry.

———

Our interaction that evening bothered me so much that I was still thinking about it the next morning. I decided to send Larry an email before leaving for my job teaching music. In the subject line I wrote: "A Brotherly Kick in the Ass."

I started out by reminding him that our *Lost and Found Code* states that: 1) We support each other toward the highest good for each brother; and 2) We call each other on our blind spots and strive to do so with compassion. I wrote that what I had to say was meant with the deepest compassion and love. Then I went for the kick in the ass:

> Are you as sick and tired of your recent mantra of self-doubt
> and self-pity as I am? You are so much better than this.
> I feel like I don't want to ask you how your teaching is going
> any more, because I am met with this same sad chorus over
> and over again. I want to offer counsel but am shut out by you.
> I don't know what to say except I believe in you and I hope
> it gets better for you.

Looking back on it now, perhaps these words were a bit heavy-handed, but my freedom to speak frankly had come from the utter honesty of communication Larry and I had shared through the years. We had never held anything back from one another. This had always been the basis of our relationship, and nothing Larry had said, even in his darker moments recently, had made me feel like I needed to soften my words or hold back my feelings from him.

I went on to remind him of the ideal of service that he'd admired so much from the teachings at the Agape Spiritual Center in Los Angeles, where we both had attended services:

I thought you were dedicated to a life of service . . . to letting
God work through you, as you, in service of children and
education. Can you see surrendering to your school's plan as a
form of surrendering to God's Plan?

I was trying all angles, hoping to throw my sinking brother a lifeline
that could pull him out. I didn't know what else to do. I finished my
note by suggesting he go back on Zoloft, the antidepressant drug he had
stopped taking several months before. On that subject I added:

I remember how good you felt when you began taking it a few
years ago. How suddenly the glass was no longer half empty
anymore. Well, my brother, all I have heard from you recently
is 'half empty, half empty . . . going on all empty.'
It helped you before. Why not give it another chance?

Finally, I concluded by asking Larry who his master was. Was it the
confusion of petty problems and worries or was he able to live for a higher
calling? Then I clicked the "Send" button and left for work.

That afternoon I got an email back from him telling me that I didn't
understand the depths of his despair. He was right. I didn't. Later that
same day he sent me another, kinder email:

I appreciate you, Bob, so much more than I sometimes show.
You are a true brother and friend and I am blessed to know
you. I love you.
Wabaawab*
Lar
(*We are brothers above all we are brothers.)

My reply:

HANG IN THERE MY BROTHER . . . Bob

That day, Thursday, October 13, was Yom Kippur, the Day of Atone-
ment and the holiest day of the year in Judaism, and my wife's daughter

and her husband had flown in from New York for a short visit. So for the next few days, I was preoccupied with family. On Friday night, Amy, my wife, cooked a big turkey dinner. She called it "Thanksgiving in October." I didn't hear from Larry over the weekend but didn't think much of it. I figured we'd had a heavy exchange and were taking a break from each other for a couple of days. I hoped he was taking the time to consider some of what I had said in the email and that we would continue our dialogue the following week.

And so began our unfinished conversation . . .

After Larry's death, I started to have feelings of regret over our final email exchange. I can't help but wonder if there was anything that I or anyone else could have done to avert his demise. However, I've eventually come to understand that, by the time Larry finally chose to end his life that fateful night, there was probably nothing that could have stopped him. But, awash with unrelenting guilt and remorse, I have a lot of further "talking" with him and with myself to get through before I can come to terms with his decision.

Disregarded Warnings
Journal Exercises

SIGNS OF SUICIDE

CONTRIBUTING FACTORS

LAST CONTACT

REMORSE AND REGRET

: Consider some of the common signs of suicide—deepening depression or dramatic mood changes; feeling hopeless, empty, or worthless; crisis in self-esteem; feelings of humiliation, failure, or decrease in performance; feelings of excessive guilt or shame; anxious or agitated; anger, rage, or self-destructive behaviors; severe loss or potential loss; feeling desperate and trapped with no way out; guilt or seeking revenge; unable to sleep/eat or sleeping/eating all the time; loss of interest; seeing no reason for living or having no sense of purpose; withdrawing from others and life; increased alcohol or drug use; reckless behavior; putting affairs in order, giving things away, or saying good-bye; talking about wanting to harm or to kill oneself; having access to a means of harm; talking or writing about death, dying, or suicide. Look back to the days and weeks that preceded your loved one's death and write about the indications that she might have been suicidal. How did you and others respond?

: What were some of the circumstances that might have contributed to your loved one's final act? Reflect on how she responded to these circumstances and how her choices affected you.

: If she had ever talked about, written about, or attempted to end her life in the past, what was your reaction? Had it crossed your mind that she could or would actually end her life in this way? Take time to express your feelings in your journal.

: Describe the last time you had contact with her. What did you do together? What was not done? Describe the last conversation you had, and what was said or left unsaid.

: One aspect of grief is called "bargaining"—trying to negotiate with reality by focusing on all of the "if-onlys": "If only *that* did or didn't happen." "If only she or I did or didn't, say or do, *that*." What are your "if-onlys"? Write them in your journal and let yourself explore the thoughts and feelings that come up with each one.

: You may want to try a "do-over" dialogue. Reflect on those times your loved one was depressed or suicidal, and what you did or didn't do for which you feel regret. Choose one of those interactions and write an interactive dialogue with your loved one, re-doing what you said or did. It may seem strange at first to be "speaking as her," but try to suspend judgment and just let it flow. Let yourself listen in your mind for the voice you knew—what might she be saying to you now? Letting yourself remember and imagining a different way can bring healing to those painful memories.

Returning to the present moment . . .

Stand comfortably and feel your feet on the ground. With an inhalation, stretch your arms overhead as you lift your spine and your face upwards. Breathe gently, then exhale and release your arms out and down.

I am present and connected to the earth.

4: Unanswered Questions

Today I put a photo of Larry on the altar in my meditation/writing room. There, among the statues of Buddha and images of compassionate Bodhisattvas, is my friend's smiling face. Taken in a bar in Atlanta, the photo shows him raising a glass in what looks to me now like a farewell toast. I recite a Buddhist prayer intended to guide the spirit of the departed. After sitting in meditation for a while, I decide to write a letter to my lost friend.

It has been scarcely twenty-four hours since I learned that Larry had taken his own life, and I can't get used to him not being around. It feels like he's away on a trip and I just haven't heard from him for a few days. My cell phone usually rang a couple of times a night with Larry calling to comment on an exciting play in a ball game or asking me what I thought about the latest episode of some televison show like *Six Feet Under, Carnival,* or *Rome.* But the phone isn't ringing now, and my mind is flooded with unanswered questions.

Why did you take those pills? I can feel my anger rising. *You jerk! Why? I love life and want to live every moment of it to my last breath. Why would you give up such a precious gift?*

I'd felt proud to tell people that in my late fifties I still had a "best friend." In my letter I tell Larry that best friends just don't do something like that to best friends. He'd given me no warning, although perhaps I just hadn't heeded the warning signs that had been there. At the very least he'd never told me in one of our heart-to-heart talks that someday he might do a horrible thing like kill himself.

And then I tell him about my Aunt Minerva. She'd been the first person in my life to speak of suicide in a positive light. I was about ten years old when she talked to me about never wanting to live in an old age home. She said that if she was ever sick or bedridden in her old age, I shouldn't think badly of her if she took her life. She let me know that it was okay under certain circumstances. She tried to prepare me. Even as a child I could understand.

Unfortunately, she was eventually confined to a bed in an old age home for years. She'd lost the ability and presence of mind to do what she said she was going to do. There was also no one there at the end to grant her the dignity of her last wish by pulling the plug. So she died the death she feared—alone, disabled, forgotten, and strapped helplessly to a bed. At least she'd prepared me.

But not you, Larry. You just left abruptly, without warning. I am still so pissed off at you. This morning I felt the welling up of tears, but I didn't let them come.

After Larry's death, I'd taken his dog home with me—Buddy, a big Black Lab/Husky mix. "Buddy Bear" Larry used to call him. Buddy always seems to be smiling, and his ears flop like he's wearing a World War II aviator's hat with the flaps down. Buddy seems happy at my place, hanging out with his doggie friend, my dog Dizzy. They sit together with their tongues out, reminding me of the "old friends . . . bookends" in the Paul Simon song Larry loved so much. At first Amy thought our house was too small for two dogs, but I wanted to keep Buddy because I feel like he is now my only link to Larry.

I find myself stroking the dense fur on Buddy's back and thinking of you, Larry. Just to touch his rich soft coat is sensory pleasure. Pleasurable, because his fur feels so good to the touch. Pleasurable, because I feel him getting so much delight from being petted. You must have experienced this. If you did, how could you have left, knowing you'd never stroke his soft black fur again?

Larry and I often would walk Dizzy and Buddy together. It was our occasion for quiet conversation and discussion, a time for taking stock of our lives and just being together. But now I am taking the dogs for walks by myself. The first time I go out with them alone is a gray, cold, and rainy October day. That seems fitting. The outer world reflects my inner state, the sky producing the tears that I don't yet have for Larry. Shock and anger still seize my gut, eclipsing the raw grief in my heart.

The dogs and I walk to Clover Park. It's early evening and the sun is just setting. The October air feels fresh and cool. Buddy and Diz are straining at their leashes. When we get home, I write to Larry.

I missed you as I held on to both of them. Walking with a good friend like you was such a simple and blessed pleasure. I suppose we both took it for granted. Now it is so strange that we will never walk together again. I just can't accept it, my brother! What was it that blinded you to this ordinary magic of daily life? I'd like to say it felt like you were walking with me and the dogs this evening, but it didn't feel like that. You are someplace else.

Unanswered Questions
Journal Exercises

CREATING A PLACE OF HONOR
WHY?!
ATTITUDES ABOUT SUICIDE
REMEMBERING SHARED PLEASURES
MEDITATION

: Create a special space in honor of your loved one where you place such things as a lit candle, a flower, sacred objects, photos, or remembrances of him. You might want to sit at this "altar" each day as you meditate or as you reflect on your loved one and your journey of healing.

: What questions about your loved one's life and death are you left with? Write a letter to him asking all the "whys" that arise in your awareness, and expressing the feelings that come with each question.

: Did your loved one feel that there were certain circumstances in which ending one's life might be acceptable? Explore his attitudes, as well as your own, about end-of-life choices when someone is in great emotional or physical pain.

: What were the everyday pleasures in your loved one's life? Write a letter to him remembering the fun and simple times you shared and the ways he enjoyed life. Notice any positive emotions you may feel in this moment. Where in your body do you register these tender feelings? Perhaps a warmth in your chest area, a softening in your belly, or a light easy smile. If tears arise, let them come, and also notice where in your body you feel the pain of grief.

: Meditating for a short period or simply sitting silently and gently breathing can quiet your mind and help you experience your grief with gentleness. This can be as brief as five minutes, but doing it regularly can bring you balance, even a sense of acceptance and peace. If sitting still is challenging, you might walk slowly and quietly, with the same intention to be present with kindness. (See Appendix 1, "Tool Kit for Your Journey to Healing" for simple meditation instructions.)

Returning to the present moment . . .

Sit quietly and allow your attention to rest with your breath. Meet whatever is arising in your mind and body with compassion. With each exhalation, feel as if your awareness is expanding outward.

I rest in this moment with compassion and open awareness.

5: DELVING DEEPER

Dear Larry . . . I am devastated and just beginning to let in that you are gone forever. I miss you terribly. Had you died tragically and suddenly from an accident or a stray gunshot I could be more in pure grief. But mixed with my sadness at your loss is my indignation and anger at you for taking your own life. It was wrong, my brother. In effect you murdered yourself. Remember the commandment, "Thou shalt not kill." I believe that murder, taking a life, even if it is your own, is wrong.

IT IS THREE DAYS after Larry's suicide, and I am wrestling with a storm of emotions—sadness, anger, regret, loneliness, and abandonment, to name just a few. This is different from the times when close relatives died from natural causes. Then I could just feel the sadness and grief of the loss. But with Larry's suicide my anger and judgment of him and his act are clouding my emotional sky.

A mixture of sadness, anger, guilt, and overwhelm is a natural part of the process of coming to terms with loss, even after a "normal" death. But a death by suicide is so devastating and deeply traumatic for loved ones that the feelings are often much more intense, more intrusive, and harder to resolve. I know that this flood of conflicting emotions is blocking my deeper feelings about the loss from coming through. I continue writing, and as I do my outrage begins to shift toward curiosity.

In your moment of resolve to die—to kill yourself—did you succumb to or did you overcome your fear, Larry? Fearlessness in the face of death is a good thing, a noble thing. But what about the fear we each must face in daily life? The fears of rejection, abandonment, being unloved? To experience fearlessness we must first acknowledge the fear. Maybe if you'd been willing to turn and face it, my friend, you could have made other choices. If you could have listened to and understood your fear, maybe you wouldn't have invested it with so much power. What looked like an obstacle could have become a doorway, allowing you to step through the fear, toward freedom. On the other hand, if you had actually overcome your fear and had attained a sense of fearlessness, why then wouldn't you have chosen to live?

I could feel my mind reaching for some spiritual meaning that could explain it all. *Perhaps it wasn't the fear at all, Lar, but the allure to merge back into the Source because the angst of being in a painful human body with an all-too-tender human heart was just too much to bear. Was it an escape into oblivion, or did you want to reboot your life for one more go-round at being human?*

I am flooded with confusion as I watch my desperate attempts to discover some shred of reason to make sense of this unfathomable reality. I phone my friend Dean, who works in a crisis intervention center with drug addicts and prisoners in Oakland. With calm reassurance, he explains that in the brains of those who are chronically depressed there may be a chemical imbalance, which impairs judgment. He asks me if Larry had been on antidepressant medication. I tell him that he had been taking Zoloft but discontinued it about eight months ago. Dean says that his Center requires all depressed patients seeking help to stay on their medication. If they don't, they are courting disaster.

After that call, I begin to understand that Larry had a disease—depression—and he chose to stop treating it. Even though Zoloft had seemed to give him a new life a couple of years earlier, stopping it and refusing to take it again was a death sentence that none of us, especially Larry, had expected. His muddled brain chemistry prevented him from seeing that he needed to resume treatment with the appropriate medication and once again seek professional help.

The disease killed you. It snuck up on you, Larry. Depression claimed your life in the same way that cancer kills. You were not unlike a diabetic who refuses to take his insulin, a smoker with lung cancer, or an alcoholic with cirrhosis of the liver who continues to drink. Your chronic depression prevented you from seeing that this illness could kill you if you left it untreated. You were blind, or perhaps in denial, as to the severity of your disease—your dis-ease, your ill-being—and so you fell victim to the insane thought that suicide held the answer to your life struggle. In the end, your light had dimmed, and you must have listened only to the darkness of your depression.

I'd been tempted to view Larry's suicide as a shortsighted means of escape. When I begin to see that it was a disease that killed Larry, I can get a glimpse of understanding for what he has done. Even knowing that, it's still hard. I'm not over the hump yet, but Dean's explanation has given me a place to start.

Delving Deeper
Journal Exercises

FEAR AND FEARLESSNESS

DEPRESSION AS A DISEASE

PHYSICAL PAIN

TREATMENT AND MEDICATION

CONTRIBUTING FACTORS

∶ Would you describe your loved one as fearful or fearless? What frightened her? Did fear keep her from living fully? Did a kind of fearlessness, perhaps to the point of recklessness, contribute to destructive behavior and eventual suicide? As she approached the very end, do you think she was afraid? Do you think she might have wanted to change her mind at the last minute?

∶ In what ways did your loved one struggle emotionally or try to manage living with mental illness? Did she suffer from the dis-ease of depression, addiction, or post-traumatic stress disorder (PTSD)? What do you know about her condition—when it started, how it developed over time? (Note: To learn about the symptoms of the mental and emotional conditions that could have led her to suicide, visit the National Institute of Mental Health website at www.nimh.nih.gov and click on "Mental Health Information—Topics.")

∶ Acute and chronic physical pain or illness can bring great suffering, especially when it is not likely to get better. To what extent did physical pain or illness contribute to your loved one's despair and decision to take her life?

: In what ways did your loved one treat or manage her dis-ease? Is there someone you can talk with about this? Was she prescribed medication, and was she taking it regularly or abusing it? You might want to find out what kind of medication she was taking and do some research as to both its benefits and the possible side effects. If she wasn't taking prescribed medication, was she self-medicating with drugs or alcohol? If so, how did that affect her behavior?

: Write a letter to your loved one exploring why she might have taken her life. Describe any distressing or self-destructive behaviors that you may first have seen as dysfunctional but that you are now able to view as a result of depression or perhaps attempts to relieve her physical or emotional pain. You may want to convey to her your deeper understanding of what might have contributed to her suicide.

Returning to the present moment . . .

Allow one hand to rest on your chest, and breathe gently and deeply into the tenderness of your heart.

May I be filled with kindness.

6. An Absence

It's a couple of days after Larry's death, and his brother Gerry has arrived from Kentucky to take care of the things in Larry's apartment and to attend to the funeral arrangements. When I first spoke to Gerry on the phone, I was taken aback. His voice is a dead ringer for Larry's, with its slight Boston accent and inflection. Gerry is a couple of years older than Larry, a doctor, and he has two grown children. His younger son Mike, a twenty-something rock bassist living in L.A., has also come to help out. A couple of years ago, his first son, Aaron, died in a tragic automobile accident at the age of twenty-one.

Larry had been very close to his nephew Aaron. He had photos of him all over his apartment. When Aaron was killed, Larry took it very hard and told Gerry that whenever he died, he wanted to be cremated and have his ashes scattered over Aaron's grave in their Kentucky family plot. Gerry tells me that's now the plan.

We've arranged to meet at Larry's apartment. When I open the vine-covered metal gate to the front garden, Gerry is just coming in from the parking lot behind the house. I'm not prepared either for how much he looks like Larry—the same balding head and glasses, but thinner with a little more hair. As I walk toward him across the garden, the first wave of real sadness overwhelms me. Though we both try to hold back the tears, we weep as we shake hands and hug.

"I am so sorry," I say.

"I know you were Larry's closest friend," he answers, looking into my eyes. "He spoke of you often and how much you and the men's group meant to him." Gerry motions up to the apartment. "Bob, he would want you to take anything that has meaning to you or the other men."

I walk up the well-known steps, through the screen door, and into the room where Larry and I and the men's group had shared so much. Where we'd watched ball games, drummed, and had deep talks. But now there is an absence—an emptiness—about the space that makes it hard for me to even enter.

The surroundings are familiar—the dust motes in the air, Buddy's half empty water dish, the smell of cigarette butts crushed out in an ashtray, and the stale odor of coffee left un-drunk in his coffeemaker. The walls are covered with Native American sacred objects—dream catchers, masks, feathers, hand drums, art—and Red Sox memorabilia, including a framed "We Win!" front page of the *Boston Globe*'s 2004 World Series edition. Devoid of my friend's presence, the place seems lost, forlorn, and uninhabitable.

I turn away from what had been—what could have been—and get down to the task at hand. I am quickly able to find everything I'm looking for—some pictures, masks, and drums belonging to our departed brother that the men of the Lost and Found will use tonight in a ceremony remembering Larry. These items will then be divided up among the group members. I pack up Larry's two large circular hand drums. Painted on the skin of one is Kokopelli, the humpbacked flute player that represents the trickster and the spirit of music to Native Americans of the Southwest. The other drum has symbols of the hunt. In the corner I spot the old Styrofoam ice cooler that holds the ritual objects of our men's group—the log covered in candle wax, sage sticks, the eagle wing we use for smudging that had been gifted to Larry from a tribe he'd visited years before. When I open the cooler, there is an envelope on top in Larry's handwriting addressed to "The Men of the Lost and Found." My heart sinks as I realize that this most likely is his final note to us. I tuck it in my pocket, gather the mementos—and myself—and walk out of Larry's home for the last time.

⁓

Before I leave the front garden, I invite Gerry and Mike to attend our Lost and Found meeting that evening. They are swamped with the apartment clearing, but Gerry says they'll try to make it. And he tells me that two suicide notes had been found by the police. One is addressed to me. The other is for Mary, Larry's ex-wife, who'd remained his closest female friend after they divorced. While he is telling me that I can get my note at the police station, Mike shows up with a copy he's just found on Larry's computer. Not wanting to read Larry's last words without the other Lost and Found brothers present, I thank him and add the note to the one in my pocket. I'll read them tonight at the meeting.

As I turn to leave, Gerry asks me if Larry had owned a gun. I have no idea, but I presume that he didn't.

"Well, we found this receipt in the glove compartment of Larry's car." He shows me a wrinkled bill of sale from a local gun shop. It shows that Larry Harpel had purchased a Berretta 9mm Px4 Storm for $250. The receipt is dated October 13, 2005, two days before Larry killed himself with an overdose of sleeping pills. Due to the California law that requires a two-week waiting period, the gun could not be claimed until October 27. Larry couldn't wait.

An Absence
Journal Exercises

YOUR LOVED ONE'S PLACE
THE MEANS
TALKING WITH OTHERS
INDIVIDUAL WAYS OF GRIEVING

: What do you remember about the place where your loved one lived or where you spent time together? As you write, pay attention to what you see, smell, hear, taste, touch, or feel as you recall being there. What were the unique things that made this his place in the world?

: How do you feel about the means your loved one used to end his life? Writing in your journal, express your feelings directly to him regarding this particular choice. Tell him what effect it had on you. Your feelings may range from anger to compassion. Let yourself tell all.

: Speak with some relatives or friends of your loved one. What do they feel and think about the suicide? What do you share with each of them about your own thoughts and feelings? Later, recall the conversations by writing them in your journal as dialogues. What insights do you gain about your loved one? About yourself? If there has been a friend or relative who you can't talk to directly about the suicide, write a letter to that person in your journal, not necessarily to be mailed, but as an opportunity to express the truth of your experience to them.

: How someone shows their grief is unique to each individual and may vary day to day. Observe the ways that people around you are dealing with their grief following such a tragic death—flooding with emotion and tears or defending against all feelings; taking care of business or being passive and withdrawn; expressing outrage or relief; longing or tormented by guilt. Write a letter to your loved one telling him how you and others who knew him have responded after his death. Remembering that there is no "right" way to grieve, notice when you are pulled to judge and when you compassionately observe each individual expression.

Returning to the present moment . . .

Take a few full gentle breaths to relax. Let your eyes close and remember a time when you felt safe and calm. As you recall, notice what you see, hear, smell, touch, or taste in this moment. Savor the good feelings in your body and mind.

I rest in this moment of safety and pleasure.

7: Farewells

Six days after his death, the men of the Lost and Found Men's Council, along with Larry's brother Gerry, meet at my home for a ceremony of farewell for Larry. As I light a fire in the hearth, I remember how much Larry loved wood fires. I bring out the wax-covered log, and before we light our individual candles, we light one for our fallen brother.

For the first time ever a woman speaks at our council—Larry's ex-wife Mary. After thanking us for loving Larry and nurturing his soul, she reads us something she has written about him. She reminds us how, "Larry was a person who was intimately involved with a love of life, of thought, and was someone who was beautifully alive. He was filled with wit, wisdom, and an ebullient laugh that said so much about his courage."

Understanding the confusion all of us are going through, she goes on. "I also offer you the possibility that his strength of heart diminished not only because of his life events, but because he had suffered from and triumphed over painful and sometimes deep depression for many years. He was not a coward. He was tired. He was not selfish. He was in the profound pain of an illness that often allows for no hope and blinds one to the love of self and, most cruelly, insists that there is no help anywhere for the sheer fatigue and loneliness that envelops those lost in its embrace.

"We may have many emotions and perhaps angry tears," she continues. "But please try to remember that he didn't do this *to* us. He needed freedom, peace, and rest, and an end to pain that I'm certain was too profound to bear. I know that when I remember him, I will remember his laugh, his intellect, his gift for writing, and all that he brought to the children he worked with who brought such wonder to him." We are very still and silent as we absorb the truth of her words.

After Mary left, my friend, we drummed and chanted your name to remember and to honor you.

"Larry . . . poetry . . . Larry . . . heart . . . Larry . . . tears . . . laughter . . . wind . . . smiles . . . song . . . passion . . . joy . . . sunset . . . sorrow . . . Larry Lost . . . Larry Found. A brother has fallen. Let us all take heed. A brother is lost . . . Let us never forget!"

As the rhythm of the chant subsided, I chose the moment to read aloud your last two letters. It was not an easy task. As I began with your letter to me, my voice choked and tears welled up in my eyes.

Beloved Bob,
Thank you for being all that anyone could ever hope for in a friend and brother. I love you deeply and eternally will.

I'm sorry, my friend, that I must leave you this way. I wish it could have been otherwise, but I just don't have it in me anymore to remain behind with my pain and sadness and disappointment. There is a constant abysmal despair that I can no longer endure.

I know that when someone dies, it leaves behind sorrow and pain and even anger. I wish that it were not so, for the idea of hurting you is abhorrent to me. Our relationship has been a rare, precious part of my life. I can only ask that you forgive me for my decision and somehow wish me well along my way.

Should an afterlife and spirit world actually be true, please know that I will do everything in my power to bless you from beyond, to guard, and even guide you.

I love you, Bob. Thanks for loving me.
WABAAWAB,
Eternally, Lar
Please . . . make sure that my beautiful dog Buddy finds a loving home.

I barely make it through reading without breaking down. My heart is pounding and I am filled with emotion as I let in his final words. Larry's last message to me is so personal and so full of deep love and sorrow that all my feelings for him come crashing in. This man whom I loved so much is really gone forever. It is so hard to comprehend what has happened.

Gratefully we all sit for a while in silence. I use the pause to wipe the tears from my eyes, take some deep breaths, and clear the lump in my throat before I am able to continue with the letter he'd written to the group.

10/15/05
My Cherished Brothers of Lost and Found,
We have traveled many roads together, and I am eternally grateful for your support and brotherhood throughout my journey. Through all the twists and turns, I have felt blessed to have known you. I love you all.

Please try to understand why I have done what I've done, and, as best you can, please bless me on whatever remains of my path.

There is nothing more anyone could have done.

It's just time for me to go home. Hold me in your prayers as, if I'm able to do so, I will hold all of you in blessing.

May peace and love follow you throughout your lives.

WE ARE BROTHERS, ABOVE ALL WE ARE BROTHERS.
In brotherhood, love, and gratitude,
Larry

We all listen to Larry's words and try to understand. We search for meaning, but it's too soon. We fumble for words, trying to make sense out of the situation, but none of us have a handle on it. Gerry offers that there are some things in life that we may just never be able to understand. There are no easy answers.

After we have all spoken a final word and blown out each of our candles, only the flame of the candle we'd lit for Larry remains. We sit together in silence, waiting to hear Larry's final words. Usually he had been the last one to "check-out" at the end of each meeting. In the lingering quiet, we feel him silently speaking to each of us in our minds and hearts.

In closing, I read part of the poem "Song of Myself" by Walt Whitman:

I bequeath myself to the dirt
to grow from the grass I love . . .

If you want me again
Look for me under your boot soles.

You will hardly know who I am or what I mean,
But I shall be good health to you nevertheless,
And filter and fiber your blood.

Failing to fetch me at first keep encouraged,
Missing me one place search another,
I stop somewhere waiting for you.

Then we all stand encircling the log, leaning in with our arms around each other, and together we blow out Larry's candle . . . *Larry, where has your flame gone?*

A few weeks before Larry's suicide, I heard a talk by the great Vietnamese Buddhist teacher Thich Nhat Hanh. He started his talk by holding up a box of matches and saying, "There is a flame hidden within this box. And when conditions are sufficient, the flame manifests." Then he struck a match and a flame sprang into its short life of heat and light. Holding up the burning match he continued, "If we have 'Buddha eyes' and look deeply, we can see that even before the match was struck the flame was already there." He blew out the match and there was only smoke. "And when the flame goes out, it's still there, only it manifests in a different form. Where has it gone? It has gone nowhere. It has merely changed its 'transformation body' and is now continuing in another form."

As I later write about this to Larry, I could hear him saying, as he often did when I tried to discuss Buddhist teachings with him, "So what's your point, Bob?" *The point is, my brother, it's possible that we are all like that flame and that you are continuing now in another form. You were born into this human body, and perhaps now you continue in a transformation body through the thoughts, ideas, and memories that still exist within every person you have touched—within each child you have ever taught or befriended, and within every one of your friends and family. You continue as a part of me and all the men of the Lost and Found Men's Council who looked into your eyes and called you brother, who shared your poetry, your insight, your speech, and laughter. If your tears, joy, and pain are ours, then your flame must be continuing to illuminate our lives.*

The men of the Lost and Found have gone home, and the fire has burned down to orange, red, and gray ashes. I sit alone scribbling these words to Larry. Buddy is sleeping peacefully at my side, and I can feel the sadness start to overwhelm me. *No, it is my love for you, the man, that overwhelms me. My love for you will never be extinguished, my brother. It is that love that I want to shout to the sky, to the winds, to the seven directions—north, south, east, west, above, below, and within. I know you are here very close to me, my brother. I hear the melody of your voice that still echoes in the silence.*

I pick up a piece of paper I'd set aside on my desk—a poem found on Larry's computer that was written the night of his suicide.

Final Poem and Testament
By Larry Harpel, 15 October 2005

I used to be able to function in the world,
But now,
I cannot make it through a day
without a sinking sense
Of despairing fatigue.

I used to cry on occasions
When everything ". . . gathered up. . . too much . . ."
But now, whether or not tears visibly flow
They are constantly flowing within.

Everything has gathered.
Everything is too much.
I am on the verge.

I used to be gifted with hope from the eyes of children,
But now all I feel is wistful and sad.

I used to think that it was
Only a matter of time

Until I discovered how
To make the whole damn thing work.

But now,
The light of possibility
Dims quickly
To imperceptibility.

I used to think I would find enduring love,
Or that it would find me.
I used to think that my salvation lay there,
Radiant in golden light,
Soft,
Comforting,
Warm.

But now,
I know better.

There is no salvation to be had from another,
Only from within,
And within is empty, deeply empty,
With depth I no longer have
The strength or
The will to plumb.
And so I die,
In the final, desperate belief
That either oblivion
Or freedom
Awaits me.

Farewells
Journal Exercises

SUICIDE NOTES

CONTINUING IN ANOTHER FORM

WORDS OF INSPIRATION

GATHERING TO SAY FAREWELL

: Not all suicide notes are as poetic as the ones my friend Larry left. Some may be incoherent, full of pain or rage. Did your loved one leave a note or final writings? If you have access to it, copy the note into your Grief and Healing Journal in your own hand. Notice and record what feelings arise in you as you transcribe. When you feel ready, write a response to her last note. If no note exists, try to compose one yourself. What might your loved one have said in a farewell note? What do you wish she might have said?

: Explore the ways that your loved one might be continuing in other forms through the people she touched and the contributions she made in her life.

: Create a special section in your journal for poems or other inspirational writings you find that express your feelings about the mysteries of life and death. Copying a poem or other writing in your own handwriting can bring you closer to the deeper meaning it holds.

: What kind of farewell gathering did you have after the death with those closest to your loved one? This might have been a funeral mass and burial, or sitting shiva, or a private ceremony or ritual. Write her a letter telling her about what you did. If you didn't have this kind of farewell, or one that you feel good about, write in your letter about what you would have done instead.

Returning to the present moment . . .

Sit comfortably with your spine long and your belly soft.
With each breath, invite ease and comfort. Let each breath be
like a warm wind or a gentle wave.

*Breathing in I relax. Breathing out I release
my pain and sorrow.*

8. Getting Real

Lar—you've been dead eight days today. Damn . . . eight days of this planet Earth being a little lighter and more empty. Seemingly endless days and nights without hearing your voice—at times a cantankerous voice but one that was always sweet to my ear. By sweet I mean the quality of love and companionship that we shared is perhaps rare for two men who were . . . okay let me say it . . . not gay, not lovers—something we never contemplated. Yet we were as close as two men could ever be.

I AM WRITING in my journal to Larry when, for some reason, I actually pick up my cell phone and push "6" on my speed dial to ring his number. He answers! He says, "Hi, this is Larry. Please leave your message after the beep. Thanks. Good-bye." Apparently his cell service hasn't been canceled yet, so I got to hear his curmudgeonly voice one last time. I almost leave a message, something like, "Lar . . . the World Series starts tonight and . . ."

Instead, I write the conversation that I imagine might have taken place between us. As I write I let myself fall into the usual back-and-forth banter I know so well from our years of friendship.

"*So, Lar, what are you up to?*"

"*Nothing. I'm just taking Buddy for a walk before the game starts.*"

"*Yeah, I know it starts in a half hour. I was wondering if you wanted to come over to my house or should we watch it at your place?*"

"*Ah . . . man, I've got to plan some lessons for school tomorrow. Do you mind coming over here?*"

"*No big deal. I'll pick up a couple cans of Guinness. Maybe we can order in a pizza later.*"

"*Yeah, sure, whatever.*"

"*I'll see ya in about fifteen minutes.*"

"Your fifteen minutes or real fifteen minutes?"

Larry used to refer to my habitual lateness as "Bob Time." Man, he used to get on my case about that.

"Really fifteen minutes. Don't want to miss the first pitch. See ya in a few."

It seems so simple and even a little silly, but creating a dialogue with my deceased buddy is rekindling a connection I haven't felt since his death. I'm finding real comfort from inventing this conversation. For a moment I'm recapturing the familiar feeling of making small talk with my best friend. Perhaps because it is so familiar to me, I am easily able to write in Larry's "voice." I decide to continue the dialogue and see where it goes. Soon it leads to a place I would never have expected.

"Psst . . . hey, Bob."

"Was that a voice?" I actually say out loud, surprising myself. Though I know this is in my imagination, I'm curious, and I continue writing.

"Yeah, hey man, it's me . . . Larry."

"Come on, get out of here. You're just a voice inside my head."

"No, man it's really me. I'm on the other side. And I can do this."

"Bull shit!"

"No man, really! This is amazing. It's me. Seriously."

"What the hell? This can't be happening. I must be losing it."

"Bob, you need to calm down. It's okay. Believe me, this is no big deal."

"NO BIG DEAL!"

"No big deal. Man, if you'd seen some of the things I've seen since I died! This is nothing honestly. No . . . big . . . deal!"

"OK, if this is really you, I've got a couple things to say. You left us all feeling really rotten about you killing yourself. Did you think about us? Didn't you realize how much what you did was going to affect us? A lot of people including myself see you as being a quitter."

"I was so tired of all the shit."

"Well, like they say, 'Shit happens!' That's no excuse. You just gave up on life."

"I just couldn't go on any more. I wanted to go home."

"All of us aren't as pissed at you as I am. Lost and Found brother Bruce says he thinks it was a courageous act. He thinks that you did what you needed to do. You'd had enough. You just didn't want to be in pain anymore."

"He's right. It was my life after all. Don't you believe in free will? I had the right to end my life whenever I wanted to."

"That's selfish, Lar."

"No, Bob, it was my prerogative. Remember existentialism? Albert Camus . . . The Stranger? He said that the ultimate choice an individual can make is whether to live or die. 'To be or not to be.'"

"Don't go quoting Shakespeare. It's fucked up, man!"

"No, I simply did what I had to do. I just couldn't go through all that suffering and pain again. You knew what it was like."

"Sure I did. I was your closest friend, remember? I went through a lot of it with you."

"But you didn't experience the pain in my arm for years without relief. That had come back. I'd had enough."

"Cut the bullshit. You could have gotten help. Pain medicine . . . a pain block."

"No more doctors! I just couldn't go through all that again."

"Hey, we each have our own personal pain. Mine's just different from yours. I've lost both my mother and father. After almost being blind with blurry triple vision for a couple years, I had two cataract operations. Then there was cancer in my thyroid, which I had removed. I've been through a couple of marriages and divorces. I had my own traumas, but I never felt like checking out. So it's difficult for me to agree with Bruce and say I think you did a noble thing . . . that you did what you needed to do. Bullshit. I think what you did was a cop-out. You did it with no consideration for anyone else. Did you realize how it would affect everyone who loved you? We the living?! I want you to know that a lot of us are still pissed off. It was a bad idea."

All that anger and pain is just flowing out of my pen. I've written before how angry I am but nothing like this. The conversation has just taken a turn naturally, like "automatic writing." It feels right to do, and I'm not about to stop or pull any punches.

There had been no "response" from Larry after my last statement so I continue to hold the floor.

"That's right, just shut the fuck up and listen to me for a change, Larry. See, I can control you now. You are just an invention of my mind. A literary conceit."

"Nope, you're wrong there. This is really happening. I can talk to you from the other side. I'll prove it. Listen. For a moment I thought I heard a metallic sound, like the ringing of a small gong.

"What the hell was that?"

"It was that brass 'singing bowl' you gave me when you tried to teach me to meditate. You couldn't find it when you cleaned out my apartment, right?"

"Yeah, that's right. I wondered where the hell that thing went. It had such a nice ringing sound."

"Well, you couldn't find it because I took it with me. You'll be happy to know that I've finally learned to meditate over on this side. It's cool, since time doesn't exist over here."

"You're dead. As dead as Boston's chance against the White Sox pitching this year."

"Yeah, three complete games against the Angels. That was pretty impressive. I am sorry I missed the final game. At least I'll always have last year, 2004. Ahhh . . . my Red Sox won it all. Man, the way they came back against the Yankees after being down three games to none in the American League Championship Series. That was sweet! Finally beating those fuckin' Yankees. Winning the series was great! I waited my whole lifetime for that. And when Boston finally won it all, I knew that I could leave this life and that a little part of me would die happy."

"I knew you were a lifelong Red Sox fan but, Lar, isn't that a little too much?"

"No, you have no idea what it was like growing up in Boston, living and dying with each swing of the bat at Fenway Park. That's why there are so many depressed people from New England. That and . . . the winters." Larry laughed. "Man, I'm serious! I'm sure there are a lot of Boston fans out there who had the feeling that when the Red Sox finally won the World Series, we had completed something we were placed on Earth to see through, and now we could be released."

"You mean after eighty-six years of Boston not winning a World Series, 'the curse' has finally been reversed?"

"That's what I'm talkin' about."

My writing comes to a conclusion just like that, as if we have each simply hung up at the end of a phone conversation. I've made my point and Larry, as usual, has had the last word. We've spoken about mundane stuff, but we also touched on deeper issues. It feels like this is the first time I've been able to express some of my pain and distress directly to him.

Immediately after, I feel a kind of relief, as if we had really just had a short visit. I realize that maybe Larry isn't as lost to me as I'd previously thought. In fact, I've discovered through writing this totally imaginary conversation that I can speak with Larry, or at least that part of Larry that still exists inside my consciousness, whenever I want. There was something very familiar and comforting about our interaction. I want to keep writing to him, because there is still so much that I need to express. This "getting real" dialogue with Larry was to become a form that I continue to explore through my journaling in the coming months and years. I've found it to be an indispensable way of rekindling and sustaining the link between us.

Getting Real
Journal Exercises

CREATING DIALOGUES

TALKING ABOUT THE HARD STUFF

GUILT AND REMORSE

UNFINISHED BUSINESS

STAYING CONNECTED

: Write an interactive dialogue between you and your deceased loved one. You might begin with a simple conversation about the kinds of things you used to talk about with him. Be spontaneous, playful, even outrageous—whatever captures the unique characteristics and nuances of your typical conversations.

: When you feel ready, let your conversation go deeper. Ask hard questions, explore differences, debate values and choices. As the dialogue unfolds, explore the disappointment, frustration, anger, and pain you both feel. Listen beneath the suffering to hear and say what you're each really trying to communicate. Whatever had been said or left unsaid, done or left undone, express it through ongoing interactive conversations.

: Getting real with yourself means noticing—with courageous honesty —your actions and feelings, even difficult feelings such as guilt and genuine remorse. Write a dialogue in which you express your regrets and see what the response of your loved one might be. Write a scenario in your journal in which you and your loved one both take responsibility, make amends, and experience deeper understanding and reconnection with each other.

: We may gain comfort from continuing the relationship with our loved one after death—from talking to those we've lost and sharing the latest family news, to the woman who used to ask her late husband, "Ed, where are my glasses?" and then she'd find them! What are the ways that you find yourself reaching out to your loved one that help you stay connected?

Returning to the present moment . . .

Stand with your knees slightly bent and your feet firmly planted on the earth. Let your spine be long and your head upright. As you breathe, feel your clarity, your truth, your unique inner wisdom.

I choose to speak and act from my inner truth.

9. Emotional Roller Coaster

ONE MORNING during meditation, the floodgates finally open and I cry uncontrollably. It has been only ten days since Larry's suicide. Every morning I've been saying a prayer to Avalokitesvara, the Buddha of Compassion, "The One who hears the cries of the world." This morning after the prayer, I bow silently to Larry's photo on my altar, and feel a welling up of tears. I bow to his smiling face and to the friend I loved. That's when the deep sobs come. They will continue to flow for several days. I find, to my surprise, a relief to finally open fully to the powerful waves of emotion.

The ancients say that the soul of the deceased travels to the other shore—the land of the ancestors—across the river of tears that we, the living, cry in our grief. This gives our grief a higher purpose. Without our tears there would be no watery passage for the departed.

The crying feels good, even healing, but then a kind of numbness and residual anger set in once again. It's as if someone has murdered my best friend, and I'm still really pissed off about it. It just so happens that the person who murdered Larry was Larry! While I feel the full weight of the irredeemable loss, I still can't accept Larry's choice to end his own life. No matter how much I try to feel connected to him, I somehow can't get over the profound break in our connection his last act created.

The psychologist Milton Erickson describes a "break in belonging" as the experience a person has when he feels disconnected from himself, from others, and from something greater than himself. I am feeling painfully cut off from Larry, a break in belonging with someone who'd been an integral part of my life. As I let in the agony of that rupture, I begin to realize that my break in connection with him must be nothing compared to what he'd been feeling during his final days and weeks. That was a separation of such magnitude that it manifested in suicide. It was an estrangement from himself so great that it resulted in the act of self-annihilation. Ending his life was a break in everything he belonged to, including our friendship.

We'd been friends for fifteen years, and Larry's act couldn't take anything away from what we'd shared. But his suicide ended our living belongingness. I still feel sad, but I notice my tears have dried up again. I seem to be on a roller coaster of feelings about Larry, and all I can do is hang on for the ride.

Emotional Roller Coaster
Journal Exercises

A Prayer for Your Loved One

Crying

Break in Belonging

Highs and Lows

- Find a prayer or compose one for your departed loved one. Set aside a certain time each day in the morning or evening to light a candle and recite the prayer, holding her in honor and remembrance.

- What is your experience of crying? What brings up or blocks your tears? How would you like to be supported when you grieve? Do you prefer to be alone or do you want to be held by someone in your sorrow?

- Reflect on how your loved one must have been experiencing disconnection from herself and others, and from something greater than herself. Write a letter to her in your journal sharing your reflections about what might have contributed to this break in belonging. Tell her how you were affected by her withdrawal, isolation, or alienation.

- Intense emotions can vary wildly after such a shocking and tragic loss. What has your emotional roller coaster been like since the suicide? Notice the full spectrum of emotions. What brings your feelings to the surface or shuts them down? Write about some different ways that you can respond when strong feelings arise. What supportive choices can you make when you feel upset or vulnerable?

Returning to the present moment . . .

Sit with your eyes softly open or closed, and gently breathe.
Notice whatever feelings are arising. You might name them (sadness,
confusion, pain) and let them be just as they are. As you breathe
and allow, they will change and pass.

As I breathe, feelings arise and pass away.

10. TRYING TO UNDERSTAND

Larry, the days have seemed to endlessly drag on since you left us so abrupt-ly. Today I was walking again with Dizzy and your furry pal Buddy, who I have nicknamed Sir Buddley Budster, "the Gentleman's Dog," because I can imagine him wearing a smoking jacket with a pipe in his mouth. Sir Buddley is such an inquisitive old chap, always investigating everything, a veritable Sherlock Holmes of a dog.

BUDDY IS THE MOST well-adjusted of any of us. He totally lives in the present, in the now. He seems to be always smiling and curious . . . and faithful. He follows me around the house all day, especially around din-nertime. When I ask him how he feels about Larry, he shakes his floppy "aviator-hat" ears, and does a kind of snort-sneeze. I thought maybe he was saying, "Larry who?" But I've heard that this snort-sneeze is a dog's way of laughing. So maybe Buddy is simply happy just to hear Larry's name! Or maybe he's saying everything's really okay.

As the dogs ran on to Clover Park's empty baseball diamond today, I watched Dizzy doing her Border Collie thing, herding Buddy, nipping at his heels, cutting him off, and circling him back. I wish you could have seen it, Lar. These are the simple everyday things I still want to share with you, my brother.

Buddy is a genuinely cheerful spirit. He's the animal helpmate of fairy tales, the friend trapped in the body of a bear or wolf, who is there to encourage and protect the hero and guide him on his quest. He has a big loyal heart and is a constant friend and companion. With a companion like Buddy at his side, Larry's self-murder is even more incomprehensible to me.

Larry, leaving Buddy is still a hard one for me to understand. Your final note asked me to be sure that your beloved dog would find a loving home. So obviously you did care, and trusted me to care as well. I just don't get it, but I am beginning to feel how deep and vast your pain and desperation must have been for you to have abandoned your furry friend like that. Just like our curious dog Buddy nosing around, I am still searching for meaning.

—

It is a clear crisp autumn day as I walk alone with the dogs along the canals in Marina Del Rey where the four of us used to go together. The sky is blue without a cloud. White sailboats travel up and down the estuary. Flocks of ducks quack comically in the canal. A lone white heron, with its killing bill pointed just above the water, waits in a silent hunting ballet pose to spear a fish. The temperature is in the low seventies.

With my senses awakened by the freshness of the day, I sit down on a park bench and silently read a few lines from the poem "Full Moon Festival" by Thich Nhat Hanh:

> What will happen when form collides with emptiness,
> And what will happen when perception enters non-perception?
> Come here with me, friend,
> Let's watch together.
> Do you see the two clowns, life and death,
> Setting up a play on stage?
> Here comes Autumn.

The bench overlooks the gentle swells of waves, and I watch the passing boats. A cool ocean breeze blows a few fallen leaves toward the water. A white-haired couple sitting next to me on the bench asks what breed Buddy is. I tell them a Husky mix and that I have recently adopted him when my friend, his master, died suddenly.

When they asked what happened, I told them that you'd died in your sleep, Larry. I can't quite yet say "suicide" to strangers.

"How old was he?" they ask.

"Fifty-five," I tell them.

"The same thing happened to my son," the old man offers, his face suddenly becoming very solemn. "He was fifty-three."

There is a long pause. We watch the white sailboats and feel the late

October sun on our faces. Then I say, "I'm sorry about your son." The old woman says, "We're sorry about your friend."

Death is so permanent, my brother. Feelings, problems, emotions, even sensations of pain are all impermanent, and transparent. Just fifteen days ago you would have been with me and Buddy and Dizzy, sitting and watching the boats, but you chose a permanent solution for your temporary woes. There are no clouds today. Above, only unobstructed blue sky. Do you see the clowns . . .?

Trying to Understand
Journal Exercises

BECOMING CURIOUS

RELATIONSHIPS WITH ANIMALS AND PETS

GRIEVING AROUND STRANGERS

TRANSFORMING SHAME

: For me, becoming a "detective" in my journaling led to new levels of understanding and healing. As you become curious, you can begin to work through the loss rather than react to it. What about your loved one's life evokes your curiosity? Look beyond the facts for underlying meaning. What still leaves you puzzled about your loved one's death? Where do you want to nose around to find answers?

: How did your loved one relate with animals or pets? In what ways was his connection with animals similar or different from his relationships with humans? If your loved one had an animal at the time of the suicide, how did the pet respond to the loss? If you cared for the pet afterward, how did this affect your grieving and healing process?

: Do you find that you feel ashamed to tell others, even friends, that your loved one took his own life? Suicide has often been hidden because of the unfortunate stigma that many people have attached to suicide, depression, or mental illness. While this is changing, notice if you feel embarrassed or disgraced as you talk about the suicide. In your journal, write about a time when you might have experienced such shame. Write a letter to your loved one telling him what it has been like to tell others about the suicide, or even to say how he died. Has this changed over time?

: In your journal, write a dialogue in which you tell a stranger or an acquaintance about the suicide and are met with understanding and compassion. What would you like to hear from the other person in this conversation? Notice the part of you that feels shame related to the suicide. Write a letter to that "shame part" of yourself, expressing your understanding and compassion for the painful feelings.

Returning to the present moment . . .

Take a short walk in a slow and mindful way, either inside or outside. With each step, feel your foot touch the floor or the earth.

With each step, I am peaceful.

11. Gaining Perspective

October has been a devastating month. Larry had given us hints that he was having a hard time, but his suicide was really so unexpected. If it had happened a year or two earlier, it might have made more sense. But this recent summer and autumn Larry seemed to have so much going for him—good friends, a support system in the Lost and Found Men's Council, his loving, loyal doggy companion Buddy, a good job at a prestigious private school in Pacific Palisades, and his new interest in exploring a spiritual practice at Agape Spiritual Center. He had found a prayer partner and had begun attending meetings, praying and meditating. He'd also met a wonderful woman there.

Two years earlier he had none of these things. At that time Larry had been on the edge, in constant pain from that first shoulder injury. At the school where he was teaching at the time, he'd fallen on the playground, shattering his elbow. The result had been months of unrelenting pain. He filed a disability case, had three unsuccessful operations, and cursed the doctors and attorneys. The pain radiated from his right shoulder down into his hand. One time he took my arm, held it in a tight hammerlock, and said, "This is how my arm feels all the time." He could hardly sleep and couldn't work.

He had a calendar on his wall on which he checked off the days left until his disability hearing, like an inmate checking off the days of his incarceration—a prisoner of his own pain. And then one day the court hearing came. He got his disability settlement. Not as much as he had anticipated, yet a goodly sum—but the pain hadn't gone away. He swore off Western medicine and turned to healers and acupuncture. With compensation and this new treatment, miraculously he appeared to be delivered. The Larry I once knew returned. I heard his familiar laugh again.

He made plans to move back to his beloved New England and use the cash from his settlement for a down payment on that farmhouse and piece of land he'd always wanted. He found a place, but because of a bad septic tank, the deal fell through. Wanting to remain in the northeast, he took a substitute-teaching job at a small public school in Vermont. It was his first time back in a classroom in three years. He became the local superstar teacher from California. The school loved him and offered him an assistant principal position. But Larry had forgotten about the darkness, cold, snow, and remoteness of a small town in the Vermont winter. He told me that he used to get up in the dark and chip the ice off his car's windshield before driving to school, and then drive home at the end of each day in the twilight to walk Buddy in the dark and bitter chill of December.

The loneliness and isolation became too much for him. When the job as a sub was over, he returned to California, ready to call it home at last. He came back because of the sunshine and his friends, and because of the solace he knew he'd find in the Agape spiritual community. I rejoiced because I thought Larry had finally found the spiritual practice he'd sorely lacked for so many years. And at Agape he met and fell in love with Kathryn. He seemed to have it all.

—

Beyond my tears there's an empty hole that had once been filled with all that I had taken Larry to be. With distance and perspective I've begun to understand that there was an underlying despondency in Larry that never got worked through; a despair that came from unresolved feelings of unworthiness and inadequacy, which manifested as hopelessness and anger. I think that's what prevented him from accepting the possibility of a fulfilling life and from really surrendering to his new spiritual practice.

The baffling part for me is that in the past few months it seemed he was coming out of his deep dark depression, but then suddenly . . . suicide. Was it an illusion that I thought my friend was opening to a new life? I'm searching for answers, but I still can't comprehend what happened. I need to find out more.

Gaining Perspective
Journal Exercises

Depression and Reprieves

But Things Were Getting Better

Further Investigations

: How were you affected by the fluctuations between times when your loved one was depressed and times when everything seemed to improve or even appeared fine? What was she like when not depressed? What situations or conditions contributed to her positive state of mind at those times?

: A suicide can occur after what seems like improvement or a recovery of more energy. There may finally be enough energy to actually act on the suicidal feelings if the underlying depression or contributing factors have not been resolved. Write what you observed about the ways your loved one appeared to rally and become more active before the suicide, or what you noticed in her steady decline until the end.

: What else do you need or want to find out about your loved one's life and death in order to gain deeper understanding and perspective? Were there lifelong patterns and feelings that she hadn't addressed that might have contributed to the suicide? You might talk about this with her in a journal dialogue.

Returning to the present moment . . .

Sit with your body upright and relaxed, and gently breathe. Observe that thoughts and feelings, no matter how difficult, come and go, continually changing. Notice that the sensations in your body also change.

With compassion I can hold even this . . . and this.

12. Transitional States

It has been almost two weeks since Larry's suicide, and this weekend I have been writing to him about something I learned from *The Tibetan Book of the Dead*. I can just hear Larry razzing me about trying to guide him through his transition after death, as the Buddhists do. But I'm finding that the wisdom of this ancient text is giving me glimpses in poetic metaphor, of what might be experienced after we die. So I write to him:

My friend, you may feel that you are sinking in water or surrounded by fire or that a tornado is striking with such force that it will destroy you and the entire Earth. You will hear the sound of a thousand thunders. But do not be afraid. Stay focused. If you don't let yourself be distracted, a mirror-like wisdom will emerge. You will cast no shadow. You will be able to travel anywhere instantaneously in thought, and you will revisit your entire life.

As I understand it, these dynamic images are really about mental and emotional states that go on in our minds every day. If we're able to see through these frightening illusions, we can begin to transcend our fear of dying. Writing this to Larry is also helping me to make sense of the powerful storms of my own thoughts and emotions, and encouraging me to go beyond my fears.

Even as Larry is transitioning beyond his life, I too am going through an in-between transitional state, or a *bardo*, as it's called in Tibetan Buddhism. I'm between life as I had known it with Larry, and my ability to live beyond the tragedy of his death. I'm facing my own demons and passing through a bardo of intense grief. I too am dying to what had been—our lifelong friendship, predictability, and my beliefs about how life is supposed to be. I'm letting go of our life together with no new ground yet to stand on.

I realize that this is an opportunity for me to see clearly the habits of my own mind that are keeping me stuck in the past, and to begin to open beyond them to a new way of being with myself and my life. I've even had a glimpse of how my connection with Larry might be able to evolve into a new form. His transition beyond life and my own transition through grief are running parallel to each other.

—

On Sunday I go to the service at Agape for the first time without Larry. We have gone so often together that it seems strange being there alone. I walk around the crowded sanctuary looking for an empty seat. Then by chance I see Kathryn —"Larry's Kathryn," the woman who had seemed to be the true love he'd been searching for his whole life. He'd found her, and then he'd suddenly given her up. Another mystery about Larry I'm trying to understand. Kathryn motions to the empty seat next to her, and I join her.

The service is magnificent. The Agape International Choir is dressed in colorful robes, their rapturous voices praising God in jubilant song. The featured guest soloist is the great tenor saxophonist Pharoah Sanders. The song is a new composition called "God of Inspiration." The choir begins with a Gregorian-like chant as Pharoah's tenor sax slowly awakens, like a powerful sleeping bird that stretches its wings and begins to soar. It ascends into the light of inspiration and love that the voices of the choir are creating. In my mind it feels like all this beautifully inspiring holy music is just for Larry.

Then Reverend Michael Bernard Beckwith begins his sermon, entitled "Vampires and Light Beings." He says we are all beings of light and that we must guard against the dark vampire forces, in our minds and in the world, that suck out our life energy. He tells us to stay in the light and warns that the vampire energies of self-doubt and worry are always there to distract and to suck us dry. It seems like the sermon is meant for Larry as well. I dearly wish he could be here. Maybe he wouldn't have succumbed to those vampire energies and forgotten that he was a being of pure light. Maybe that would have saved him, kept him alive.

Before the service ends, Reverend Michael announces Larry's passing. He says, "We recognize that Larry Harpel has shuffled off this mortal coil. Be at peace, Larry. Peace. Be still . . . peace. Be still."

Tears well up as I look over at Kathryn, and we begin to cry. I put my arm around her, and her body heaves in great sobs throughout the rest of the service. Our shared love for Larry has drawn us together today in the midst of the crowd, and we are able to be there for each other in our grief. Kathryn had been deeply in love with Larry and ready to spend the rest of her life with him. What the hell went wrong?

As Kathryn and I sit there, remembering this man we both had so loved, I think about what I'd written to Larry the day before. *During this next stage of your transition you will once more experience all the frustration, anger, disappointment, hope, and despair that you did in life as you reexperience all the joys and follies of your human existence. But remember these are only the projections of your own mind. You may be confronted and tormented by both wrathful and peaceful deities as you were confronted and tormented during your life by your anger and the promise of love that receded from you as you grasped for it.* The promise of love. For Larry that had been Kathryn . . . and then it was over.

When my attention shifts back to the Agape service, Reverend Michael is speaking about people being haunted by their past—by past failures, hurt, and pain. He's pointing out how some people are obsessed with the past. He says, "It really isn't the past that haunts us, because the past is actually dead and gone. It's our limited idea of the past, which we experience in the present, that brings us down. It's our present mind being constantly dragged back into what *was*, rather than living what *is*, that paralyzes us."

He concludes by saying that this obsession with the past is merely a smoke screen set up by the ego to distract us from the contract we made before we came into being—the contract to be our authentic selves. Being haunted by the past is a distraction from our soul's mission, which is, as Reverend Michael puts it, "The call from our tomorrow to do greater things." *Larry, I only wish you could have been there to hear him. But you weren't. And you won't be.*

———

Later that afternoon I find myself sitting on my back porch in the setting sun, again writing to Larry, connecting with him in his transition and at the same time healing myself with the ancient Tibetan words to the dead.

Be sure to watch for the lights, my brother. They will help you choose your rebirth. *If you stay with the white light, you will be led to the god realm. The red light will take you to the realm of the demigods. The blue light will guide you to rebirth as a human. Stay away from the yellow light for that leads to rebirth as a hungry ghost with the endless cravings of greed, envy, and jealousy, as well as addiction, obsession, and compulsion. If you want to come back as Buddy's animal brother, look for the green light but remember, though they may seem noble, animals are usually enveloped in the thick darkness of ignorance and fear. Avoid all smoky lights for these will lead you to the hell realm.*

It is advised to go for the higher realms, Larry. So if you have a feeling of climbing, that's a good thing. If you feel like you're descending, it's down to the hungry ghost, animal, or hell realm. I say go for the blue lights again, my brother—the human form that provides us with the unique opportunity to grow spiritually, through all the countless joys and sorrows, toward the possibility of enlightenment and freedom.

Transitional States Journal Exercises

BEING IN-BETWEEN

NEGATIVE AND POSITIVE INFLUENCES

THEIR SOUL'S MISSION

AFTER DEATH BELIEFS

PEACE . . . BE STILL

: Consider the in-between state—the *bardo*—that you are in now. What are you leaving behind of life as you knew it with your loved one? What demons related to the suicide are you struggling with—anger, disappointment, judgment, guilt? What can you let go of in order to open to a new life and a different connection to your loved one?

: In your journal, make a list of the "vampires" in your loved one's life that may have sucked out his life energy—work, stress, worry, self-doubt, difficult relationships, problems that seemed unsolvable.

: Write about the "Light Beings" in your loved one's life—the people or spiritual leaders who inspired him and lightened his spirits. How was he affected by them? What awakened in him a sense of reverence, awe, or connection to something greater than himself?

: As you reflect back on your loved one's life, what do you think was his "soul's mission?" How did he fulfill that mission during his lifetime through his unique vision, actions, or contributions? What distracted him from that mission?

: What are your personal and spiritual beliefs about what happens after death? Select a passage from a favorite spiritual book and read it to your loved one. Write a letter to him, or a dialogue, telling him some of the wisdom or teachings you wish he could have heard and taken to heart.

: Write a poem to your loved one on the theme "Peace . . . be still."

Returning to the present moment . . .

As you inhale, tighten your hands into fists. As you exhale, allow your hands to open and relax. Notice the difference in your body and mind between holding on and letting go.

Letting go, I am free.

13. Revealing the Shadow

On Halloween, or All Hallow's Eve, it's said that the dead walk among the living. As darkness falls on this first Halloween after Larry's suicide, I find myself wondering about what had haunted him during his final months. *Are you with me tonight, Larry? Make no mistake, my brother, there is power in this night.*

In my neighborhood in Santa Monica, it's a cool clear evening with no moon at all, and little children are coming in droves to the doors of houses all up and down the block in search of candy.

I wonder how the kids from the fourth-grade class you taught so briefly this fall are doing tonight. I wonder what costumes they're wearing. Your passing surely put a damper on some of their Halloween plans this year. Those kids won't soon forget the caring ways you touched their lives and hearts.

This night of disguises and altered identities brings to mind a ceremony the men of the Lost and Found group created two years ago at our Zaca Lake retreat. As part of our investigation into the "shadow side" of our personalities, we had each made a mask.

You were there, Larry. Your mask was a brilliant and theatrical cross between a sad clown face and a skull. It seemed filled with both light and dark humor. What was behind your mask?

We'd studied psychologist Carl Jung's theory about the shadow representing the parts of the self that we don't like to look at, the parts that we hide from others and from ourselves. The poet Robert Bly says the feelings we're ashamed of get hidden away in a "long bag we drag behind us from childhood that contains all the rejected parts of ourselves we dare not let anyone see." We stuff this bag with our anger, fear, and shame. We pack it with greed, lust, jealousy, and self-loathing. On top of that, we throw in our lies, resentment, blame, and despair. Then they turn on us. As Bly says, "Every part of our personality that we do not love will become hostile to us."

The masks we made represented our own shadows, everything about ourselves we didn't accept, everything we'd stuffed into our long bags.

The clown/death mask you created, Larry, spoke to me of your shadow—anger. "People just don't get my passion," you used to tell me. "Especially women . . . they get so afraid of me when I raise my voice. That's just how I express my passion. What's a little yelling, for Christ sake!" But your explosive outbursts cost you jobs and lost you relationships. What you called anger really masked many deeper emotions—your pride, disappointment, frustration, and layers of insecurity, guilt, sadness, and deep grief. You were tormented by fears of betrayal and abandonment.

In the shadow work we did in the Lost and Found men's group, healing ourselves meant embracing our wholeness, including the denied parts. We created masks to help us face and accept our difficult and forbidden feelings and behaviors. The intention of the evening at Zaca Lake was to discover that the repressed parts of our personalities have enormous positive power if we're brave enough to bring them into the light and allow ourselves to change.

Before we made our masks, we read aloud the words of Jungian psychologist James Hillman, who says that sometimes caring for and healing our shadow may mean simply carrying it with us consciously. As I look back on Larry's anger-shadow, I think of what the Buddhist master Thich Nhat Hanh says about how we must care for our anger the way a mother cares for her crying baby. When the energy of anger comes up, we can mindfully comfort and cradle it. That way we might look deeply into it and understand its causes and conditions before we do or say anything.

You resisted that kind of deep looking, Larry. "Anger is a good thing," you would insist. "When I'm mad, I need to express it . . . get it out." You never saw the value of exploring the anger, which would have been a way of peering behind the mask to find out what might be revealed. When you just exploded, slammed your fist on the table and shouted, you were not allowing yourself to feel the underlying feelings and unmet needs that fueled the anger. Those unfelt emotions, if leaned into, held the potential for self-awareness, healing, and transformation. Those underlying feelings could have pointed the direction toward creating what truly mattered to you.

Instead, for years you carried your anger around with you and stuffed it into the "shadow bag" of your subconscious. There was the anger from your childhood against a mother for whom you were never enough. The anger against a government who led us into unjust wars. Anger against a society that didn't understand or care about you. Anger from failed relationships. Anger from your stymied acting career. Anger. Rage. A mask.

———

As dusk fell on Zaca Lake, each of us put on his shadow mask, picked up his drum, and walked about a quarter of a mile up the trail to a clearing where, generations ago, the Chumash Indians had planted four giant oak trees in the four directions for ceremonial purposes. By the time we'd arrived and were ready to begin our ceremony, it was close to midnight. The sky above was clear and exploding with stars and galaxies. We agreed to keep our masks on for the entire ritual. We were to become our shadows for this night.

We sang, danced, and drummed for what seemed like hours. As the evening progressed, the masks seemed to come alive and change. Our dark sides unexpectedly began to transform, motivating each of us to define the meaning and direction of our lives. For me, I began to realize that my search for purpose—and my way of manifesting it—is what makes my life meaningful. I find my inspiration in the kind of music, dance, and poetry we were sharing that weekend. And I recognized that I had already been living this purpose for many years with my students as a teacher of creative arts.

That night, two years ago, Larry had been right there with us in his quest for meaning. He was ecstatic and exuberant in his passionate drumming and dance. I was secretly hoping that the passion and meaning he connected with in the ritual would help him rediscover his purpose and that he would return to his calling as a gifted teacher.

As we continued to drum and dance under the moonlight, we celebrated the wholeness we felt in claiming our shadows. Debbie Ford, author of *Embracing Your Darkside*, articulates the transformative experience we were opening ourselves to that night:

You must go into the dark in order to bring forth your light. When we suppress any feeling or impulse, we are also suppressing its polar opposite. If we deny our ugliness, we lessen our beauty. If we deny our fear, we minimize our courage. If we deny our greed, we also reduce our generosity. Our full magnitude is more than most of us can ever imagine.

I thought all of us there that night were beginning to open to "our full magnitude." I guess I was wrong.

A few days after that first Halloween without my friend, I tell the Lost and Found brothers that remembering the Zaca Lake mask ritual has allowed me to see clearly for the first time that it was Larry's shadow that killed him.

Regardless of your passionate participation in our ritual two years ago, Larry, you continued to live in fear of your personal shadow and were never able to embrace your full humanness. Accepting your dark side would have meant opening to and inquiring into the hidden aspects of yourself—your rage and fear, your loneliness, your self-rejection and perceived failures. It would have meant re-membering those split-off parts to reveal your wholeness. During the years of our friendship, you held those personal demons at bay. If you had truly understood and faced them, the knowledge of your darkness would have eventually made you stronger. Your shadow bag grew longer with each rejected part of yourself. In the end, that long bag became such a heavy burden that you thought the only way out was to escape from it by killing yourself. To embrace and transform your shadow was the opportunity never taken.

Brother Bruce calls this "the Beast-within that wants to destroy all that we hold dear." That Beast inside you, Larry, raised its ugly head and said, "You are unworthy." And you believed it, not understanding that you can't always trust what a depressed mind tells you. You mistook the Beast's words of denial for God's denial, and you succumbed to the delusion that the only escape was a handful of pills—a one-way ticket on the Oblivion Express.

Larry, your shadow was not something to be feared. Ignoring and denying your dark side only created more shadow. There was a way you could have

inquired into and transformed those feelings and behaviors and been liber-
ated from their oppression. But no. Instead you snuffed out your light. If you
had faced the darkness, you might have been able to live your whole truth, to
fulfill the promise of your inherent goodness, to honor your intelligence, and
to know that you would be guided by love. You would have been able to say,
"Where there is darkness, I will bring light."

Revealing The Shadow
Journal Exercises

YOUR LOVED ONE'S SHADOW

GIFTS OF THE SHADOW

EXPLORING YOUR OWN DARK SIDE

- To try to understand the hidden forces that contributed to the suicide, write a letter to your loved one reflecting on her shadow side:

    - What feelings, behaviors, and self-limiting beliefs made up her shadow?

    - What life circumstances may have contributed to the development of her shadow?

    - How did her shadow influence her choices, actions, ways of coping, and eventual suicide?

    - What aspects of her shadow did you accept or have difficulty with?

- Now continue the letter, telling her what you saw were the gifts embedded in her shadow side. For example, in anger, the gift might be juiciness and passion. In sadness, depth and sensitivity. How did she use these gifts in a positive way?

- In your process of healing, it can be helpful for you to consider your own shadow. Journal about any self-limiting beliefs and self-destructive behaviors that the loss of your loved one may have brought up in you. How might you more fully explore and transform your shadow to bring forth the "full magnitude" of your own light?

Returning to the present moment . . .

Notice what happens in your body and mind when you think
of a way in which you limit yourself or hold back your life.
Breathe in and fill that place with light.

I breathe in light. I send out my light.

14. Gathering to Remember

IT'S A LITTLE MORE than a month after Larry's suicide, and we are holding an intimate gathering of his friends and family to honor him. It is a beautiful, clear, and unusually warm November Sunday afternoon as we gather in Lost and Found brother Jeff's garden in the San Fernando Valley. We put folding chairs in rows on the lawn. The freshly mowed grass smells sweet, and the roses are still in bloom. I've brought a sound system and choose to play the sound track from the film *March of the Penguins* for background music. I feel that a part of Larry I knew and respected had something in common with the indomitable spirit and heart of those remarkably resilient birds.

Later I would describe the gathering to Larry. *For a podium, I placed a music stand up front with a picture of you and Buddy on it. Your ex-wife Mary brought cookies, turkey wraps, and sodas. Buddy was running around on the grass sniffing, wagging his tail, and licking a little girl's face. A collection of your photos was scattered on a table, along with scrapbooks full of pictures of you surrounded by the smiling faces of the many children you taught throughout the years.*

One by one we go up to the microphone and share anecdotes and little "Larry moments" that we remember. *You were so loved!*

Mary has us smiling as she fondly recalls Larry's inquisitive stubbornness when, on a trip to Alaska, he had become so fascinated by watching bears feed that she had to threaten divorce to prevent him from going any closer.

Larry's oldest friend Steve, who'd been his classmate at Boston Latin High School, recalls how they'd gone to Woodstock together in 1969. Steve brings out his guitar and sings the Simon and Garfunkel song "Old Friends/Bookends" that Larry so loved: "Time it was and what a time it was . . . a time of innocence." *How true that is, my brother. How could we ever have known it would come to this for you.* The verse goes on to say:

"Preserve your memories, they're all that's left you."

As I settled into the music, the words of the song struck a note deep within me. We were preserving our refelctions of you, Larry, because all that's left for us are photographs and words . . . and countless memories.

Chris, the head of the school where Larry had taught, speaks about him as an amazing teacher. She says she knew he'd been feeling overwhelmed, but she'd had confidence in him. It turns out Chris was the person who found Larry that Monday morning. When he didn't show up for work, she drove to his apartment, remembering that once when there was a power outage, Larry couldn't get his car out because the parking lot gate wouldn't open. She thought maybe it had happened again . . . .

This time she stood on your porch and phoned you. When she heard your cell ringing inside your apartment without being answered, she got worried and called the police. Chris wasn't angry but shocked that you took such drastic action. Her big worry was about how the kids would react. They were devastated by your death, even though they weren't told that you took your own life. The school had grief counselors who worked with the children, and your students wrote poems and letters to say how much they missed you.

The men of the Lost and Found also stand and speak. Cory says Larry was like an older brother to him and that Larry's boldness was a trait he was trying to emulate. Jeff shares a memory from Larry's time as an actor. "Larry told me that it pissed him off when directors would tell him that he was too 'big' in a scene, that his emotions were projecting too strongly. But that's how Larry was. He was a passionate guy."

When it's my turn, I walk to the music stand and pause to look into the eyes of those who loved Larry so dearly. I explain that I'd written my eulogy *to* Larry rather than *about* him. And it isn't exactly a eulogy. It's more of a "I-come-to-bury-Caesar-not-to-praise-him" sort of speech. I tell them that it's an honest statement of my feelings and what I have to say to Larry. Speaking directly to him, I begin:

"Larry, my hope is to approach this memorial with the same frankness that we maintained in our relationship. The agreement upon which our friendship was based was to be brutally honest with one another. If either of us didn't speak our mind truthfully, we would do so at the risk of betraying the friendship. So you and I held nothing back from each other—or so I thought. I will not change that now. My enduring love for you will never be sacrificed by false words idealizing or deifying you.

"Larry . . . what the fuck, man?!

"I have to say that I was shocked and appalled when I learned that you had killed yourself. What really pissed me off was that you left our conversation unfinished. You didn't complete it with your last brutal act, but rather by removing yourself from our connection, you left it dangling.

"Our fifteen-year conversation was about life and love, poetry and politics, women, sex, and baseball. Our conversation was about letting wisdom and compassion express through each of us. Our conversation was about beauty and light and creativity. Our conversation was about saying 'Yes' to life and to the passion of being alive. Our conversation was about living a life of service to the highest good. Our conversation was about manifesting our power and getting out of our own way. And the ball was definitely in your court, my brother. Now there is only silence."

I go on to express my anger and grief that Larry has left our long conversation unfinished, and I end with: "I refuse to eulogize you as a great man fallen . . . but being true to our personal code, I would more candidly say that you were a fool, not unlike the rest of us, and that upon occasion you shone with the brightness of a Polaris. But I suppose in the end you were just a man—'glory, jest, and riddle of the world.'"

With tears welling in my eyes and heart, I end my eulogy by reading the last part of Alexander Pope's "An Essay on Man," where that great quote appears. Pope's description of man as "darkly wise, and rudely great" seemed apt for the Larry Harpel I knew and loved. The poet's words spoke of Larry's perils and promises better than I ever could:

> Know then thyself, presume not God to scan;
> The proper study of mankind is man . . .
> Born but to die, and reasoning but to err;
> Alike in ignorance, his reason such,
> Whether he thinks too little, or too much;
> Chaos of thought and passion, all confused;
> Still by himself abused, or disabused;
> Created half to rise, and half to fall;

Great lord of all things, yet a prey to all;
Sole judge of truth, in endless error hurled;
The glory, jest, and riddle of the world!

As I gaze across the gathering of Larry's friends and family, their moist eyes and nods of agreement say it all. Later, many thank me for my candor. They say I'd given voice to thoughts they'd had, and my honesty has given them permission to no longer hold back similar feelings of disappointment and anger, as well as affection and love.

After all the guests have left and the sound system is broken down and packed in my car, after all the good-byes have been said, and the leftover coffee thrown out, I drive away with an empty aching feeling of having lost something that can never be replaced. Riding down the Ventura Freeway with Buddy leaning his head out the side window, all I can think is that my best friend Larry is gone and that none of this is ever going to bring him back. While Buddy sniffs the air and lets his ears flap in the wind, I cry silent tears.

Gathering to Remember
Journal Exercises

REMEMBERING OR CREATING A MEMORIAL

THE UNCENSORED EULOGY

: If you held a memorial, write to your loved one describing what it was like. What parts of the memorial had special meaning for you? What parts were difficult? Were there any parts you enjoyed? Was anything missing? If so, what would you like to have seen happen? Include personal anecdotes that were shared during or after the memorial.

: If you didn't have a memorial, consider holding one by yourself or with one or more people who knew your loved one. Even if it's now years after the suicide, creating a memorial or ritual can be an important part of your healing process. Gather together photographs and other mementos that capture his life. You might want to compile them into an album of remembrance. Choose the music, readings, poetry, and personal stories to honor him at the gathering.

: Write or rewrite a eulogy for your loved one. A eulogy traditionally is a speech in praise of the departed. But in this exercise you can open up the boundaries and let yourself say everything you want to say about him, and later you can decide if you want to share any of it with others.

Returning to the present moment . . .

Relax your body and breathe gently.
Recall something or someone you are grateful for.

I breathe out gratitude.

15. Abandoned

I HAD A DREAM about Larry last night. I dreamt that I'd gone back to his apartment for the last time. Everything had been cleared out. We'd shared so much time there, watching ball games on TV, eating dinner together, and having our men's meetings. But without rugs, furniture, books, or pictures on the wall, the place was soulless, vacant and empty.

On waking, I'm deeply sad and feel the need to share the dream with Larry in my journal.

I went back to your bedroom, and there was only an old bare mattress on the floor. There you were, asleep on it. I woke you up. You looked like a homeless person—a squatter—seeking refuge in a vacant flat. You were sunburned from being out on the street. You looked destitute and hopeless. I was incensed to learn that you had been holed up here in your vacant apartment ever since your death. I said, "Larry, what the hell are you doing here? We all thought you were dead."

"I've been hiding out," you said, and you explained how you had faked your own death. "I wanted to run away to a place where no one could find me, so I pretended to be dead," you told me.

I was furious with you. "You son-of-a-bitch! How could you do this to all the people who loved you! We were all devastated by your suicide and now you tell me it was all just a ruse?"

You looked at me sheepishly and said you didn't know what else to do.

I said, "Man this is the last straw. You are a pathetic jerk. You know that?!"

I told you I was through with you and walked out the door.

I don't entirely know what this dream might have been about—maybe partly me wishing Larry was still alive—but I do know for sure that it was about how betrayed and abandoned by him I feel. After his suicide, a recurring phrase that would often come to mind was, "How could you do this to me?!" So in my dream I walked out on him, just like he had walked out on me.

When you finally find a friend who really *gets* you, there is an unspoken compact that goes something like: "We are both in this together." When you share this depth of intimacy with somebody, there is the implied hope that you'll always be there for each other as you walk through life and grow old together.

Larry, how could you just walk away from fifteen years of friendship? We shared a common worldview. You and I could talk to each other about certain parts of our lives that we couldn't share with anyone else. We held nothing back. It just made life a lot more livable, pleasant, and manageable to have a friendship like ours. We were definitely there for each other. There to hang out with, to complain with, to marvel at baseball with, to read poetry with, to fight with, to go to a movie or a game or play pool or get drunk, or just look at women with, or gripe about women with, or sing the praises of women with, to do "reality checks" with. I sure wish you would have checked with me about your last decision.

I would never have given up our friendship. And that's where the abandonment issues grip my gut. You abandoned our friendship! There, I've said it! You abandoned "us" and left me here alone . . . without someone like you, who got me like you did. Without someone like you who sometimes told me to just shut up when I was talking too much. Who I was able to communicate with on a higher level and always got honesty and truth and no bullshit in return.

Corny as it may sound, it would have been nice to be those two old guys in the "Old Friends/Bookends" song, sitting on a bench and sharing their octogenarian wisdom with one another, commiserating about the world around them no doubt continuing to go to hell in some newfangled hand-basket. I always thought one day I'd be that old man with you, my brother.

A wise elder once told me that I'd be lucky if by the end of my life I'd be able to count the number of true friends on the fingers of one hand. I have one less to count now.

Abandoned
Journal Exercises

REFLECTING ON DREAMS

BETRAYAL AND ABANDONMENT

REMEMBERING THROUGH A SONG OR POEM

- If you dream about your departed loved one, write to her about it. Tell her the details of the dream and any insights you might have about it. If you don't normally recall your dreams, try putting a pencil and paper by your bed at night and just before going to sleep, resolve to dream and to remember it. Writing down even short fragments encourages better recall of future dreams.

- Pondering what a dream might be telling you can be deeply healing. There are many methods of dream interpretation, but one that you might find helpful is seeing each character in a dream as an aspect of your own self. Write the full dream from the perspective of different characters, and pay attention to what those characters are saying to you. You may discover this through writing a dialogue with them. As you explore, you might begin to understand more about the meaning of the dream for you.

- In what ways did you feel betrayed and abandoned by your loved one during the course of your relationship? What are some ways she may have felt betrayed or abandoned by you? By others? See if you can feel compassion for the pain both of you have felt. As painful recollections arise, breathe gently and with each exhalation, release the pain and anguish connected with those memories so you don't get stuck in them.

: Find a song, poem, story, work of art, or other artistic expression that you associate with your loved one. Write the words in your journal or include a copy of the image. What might this creative expression have meant to her? Listen to the song, or take some time with the words or image, and as thoughts or feelings arise, write down your reflections.

Returning to the present moment . . .

Notice any painful memories that might be in your mind right now.
As you gently breathe out, release the pain and anguish.
Let your body relax.

I love and accept myself as I am.

16. Missing Pieces

*How can I tell the story of you and Kathryn, a story of longing for love, of love
found and then lost. In many ways it's the missing piece for me in the puzzle
of your life during your last few months. I am writing this to understand, to
try to solve the mystery of what happened, so I can begin to heal and forgive.*

SINCE HIS DIVORCE five years earlier, Larry had searched for and
bemoaned the lack of a woman's love in his life. It was his constant pre-
occupation. He'd say to me things like: "If I just had a woman I could love
and who loved me . . . ." "I want to look into a woman's eyes and see her
looking back at me with tenderness and understanding." "I just want to
find a woman who will really see me for who I am, a woman who really
gets me." But he wasn't just talking about it. He was proactively searching. He made his video pitch and listed himself with Great Expectations
dating service. He went to dozens of "speed date" evenings, where participants rotated from table to table, meeting and greeting a potential
date for five minutes before moving on to the next. He did online dating. Occasionally, he even had casual sex, though that was not his prime
objective. But time and again he came up empty, returning home from
one date after another feeling lonelier and more desperate for love and
affection than if he'd never gone out in the first place.

And then along came Kathryn. They met in a prayer and study group at
the Agape Spiritual Center. After the first class Larry called my cell. "Bob,
I've just met a woman . . . or rather, this amazing woman came up to me
in the parking lot as I was getting into my car and introduced herself. I
noticed that she'd been staring at me in class all night. And we'd made eye
contact a couple of times, but I didn't think anything of it. Anyway, after
class she comes up to me and says, 'Larry, I can't take my eyes off you.' And
she gave me her number and told me to call her."

"Well, are you going to call her?" I asked.

"Hmm, I don't know. I'm so sick of dating."

"But dude, she's spiritual, and she came to you. She even gave you her number. Are you crazy? Of course you're going to call her."

"I suppose you're right. She did come up to me."

"Yeah . . .?"

"And she has these amazing deep brown eyes."

"Uh huh . . .?"

"Okay, I'll call her."

He came back shouting her praises. "She's fantastic! She's beautiful! The way she looks into my eyes is incredible! This could be *The One!*"

Kathryn was a woman you felt you could explore a relationship with as a spiritual journey, a mutual search for the God inside each of you. Kathryn had everything going for her. She was literate, intelligent, and a great conversationalist. She was a caring single mom with grown kids, and committed to her job as a therapist counseling victims of domestic violence. Besides all of these things she was petite and lovely. A stylish dresser. A real looker. A dark-haired beauty with a killer smile. And, most of all, she really dug you.

When Larry got a summer job as a park ranger at Culver City Park, Kathryn used to stop by the park on her way to work some mornings just to give him a kiss. He told me how soft and scrumptious her "honey kisses" were. "This woman really knows how to kiss," he said. "All I want to do is kiss her over and over and over again. I really don't care if we ever have sex. I'm in no hurry. Kissing is enough."

And then one evening—*was it on her doorstep or at the garden gate below your tiny Westminster flat in Venice?*—just after a good night kiss she looked into your eyes and asked you, "Are you ready for me to fall in love with you?"

That stopped you cold. You were stunned and didn't know what to say. After thinking about it for a moment, you told her, "I guess we'll just have to wait and see when that happens." But, my blind brother—it had already happened.

—

The very next weekend the Lost and Found men went on our annual Zaca Lake retreat. We noticed a change in Larry, a revitalization. He shared with us how he had told Kathryn that he would wait until she was ready for them to sleep together. Larry had chosen "passion" as the weekend's theme and led us in a wild, life-embracing dance. Not surprisingly, a week later he told us, "The deed was done."

And you once again rejoiced in the simple joys of human sexuality. Man and woman becoming one in the union of love and compassion. She was a perfect fit. She was a tireless lover. With her, the foreplay to orgasm flowed like the coming of spring to the barren winter landscape that was your body before Kathryn, and you celebrated the resurrection of your sexuality. "I feel like a man again," you told me. "I'm back! And it's all due to Kathryn."

Then, after a sleepless night in mid-August, Larry bought a dozen red roses and showed up at Kathryn's doorstep at 6 a.m. one morning. *That's when you told her that you loved her. You had spoken the "L" word. I was so very happy for you.*

And then came the unraveling.

In early September Kathryn invited you to a wedding. Together, you went shopping to pick out a new brown suit. Shopping with a woman at your side was new. You remembered shopping with your mother when she used to pick out your clothes. Was that what reignited the fear within you? You started feeling that Kathryn was trying to make you into a new you.

She also wanted to help you redecorate your apartment. Spruce it up. Give it a new paint job. You went together to pick out paint swatches. I saw them around your place. The colors were light and bright. I helped you build two new bookcases. You were cleaning up your place for her. A new life was beginning.

But then the weekend of the wedding came, and suddenly you canceled. When I came by your apartment that Monday to watch the Angels baseball game, you told me that it was over between you and Kathryn. I was shocked.

I asked you what happened.

"I suppose it was about her wanting to fix up my place. I started thinking, 'Who am I doing this for?' Sure, I wanted to clean up my place, but was it for her or me? And trying on the suit for her felt weird. Like she was trying to make me over."

"Your apartment does tend to be pretty messy, Lar. And hey, you needed a suit, man. I think it was cool that she helped you pick it out."

"I know it's in my head. But I want her to accept me just as I am. I like my apartment, dust balls and all. And, if I am going to fix it up, I want to feel that I'm doing it because *I* want to do it, not because she disapproves of who I am and how I live. I want her to just accept me for *me*. This is who I am!"

"You are going to break up with this fabulous woman, this woman who you said might be *The One* . . . you are going to break up with her over friggin' dust balls? You are out of your mind!"

"No, it's more than just dust balls . . . ."

—

And it *was* more than dust balls, as I would later find out when I talked with Kathryn, but by that time neither of us could do anything about it. Larry was gone.

"There was a darkness that hung like a pall over his apartment," Kathryn told me when we met to talk. "It freaked me out. We used to have such great happy times when we went out or he came to my place. But the darkness of that little Venice apartment totally inhibited me. It was oppressive. I certainly didn't feel like making love to him in that place. It was the darkness of his past, of his sorrow, and he was still carrying it around with him. I wanted to help him change it around. Brighten it up. Make it new. But in the end that darkness just dragged him down.

"I remember the last time I went over there," Kathryn went on. "He greeted me in jeans and an old dirty Red Sox sweatshirt. He wanted me to go on a walk with him and his dog before we went out on a date. I guess I must have given him a strange look. Perhaps he felt judged. He just stood there looking back at me as if to say, 'This is me. What you see is what you get.' And I knew that he wanted me to just accept that darkness . . . but I couldn't. It was only one part of who Larry was. I loved him, but I wouldn't let myself be dragged into his depression, because I had already been there. I have struggled to extricate myself from that kind of life, and I wasn't going to get pulled back into it.

"When we went shopping for that suit, Larry stood there for the longest time staring at himself in those triptych mirrors. Three images of this handsome, self-assured middle-aged man stared back at him. Finally, he said, 'Is this really me?' I said, 'Yes, it is, darling. You look like the man I love who deserves the best. A man who can accomplish anything he puts his mind to.'

"Then he said, 'I don't know . . . It's gonna take some time for me to get used to this. It sure feels different.'

"Our love could have done miracles," Kathryn added, "if he would have only believed in it and let it be. But he just wouldn't get the help he needed to heal through his pain. He wasn't willing to go through the fires of transformation, and there was nothing I could do to change that."

Perhaps when you got too close to actually embodying that handsome, powerful, confident, good-looking guy that you were, when you got that close to having everything you'd ever wanted, those old voices inside your head came back telling you, "No, you can't do this. You are unworthy of stepping into a life so wonderful. You are not good enough. You don't deserve such happiness." Even as you and Kathryn dreamed of creating a life together, the dust balls and cobwebs of your past came back to haunt you. When you listened to the devaluing echo in your head that told you that you were not worthy of Kathryn, not worthy of a good life, you allowed yourself to be fooled by your own mind. You got hijacked by your past.

Standing in front of the mirror in that suit, in his brief moment of potential glory, he let doubt in. And while great doubt sometimes leads to great faith, in the moment of decision, a warrior who allows doubt to twist his purpose can become lost.

I want to scream at you, "No, Larry, don't listen. The voice is lying. Don't listen!" But it's too late. And so The Brown Suit hung in your closet on that fateful night when your self-doubt finally did you in!

Instead of going to the wedding with Kathryn on that Sunday, Larry played softball and reinjured his right arm taking a swinging strike at a ball. I don't know if it was an overswing taking out all of his aggression and heartache, but it was that arm injury that plagued him in the last weeks of his life. This pain from which he could get no relief left him sleepless night after night. It was that injury, so reminiscent of what he'd suffered throughout the three years of his disability case, that I know was a major factor contributing to his demise.

So you had six weeks with the love of your life, and then that was that? You just didn't want to live with physical pain and the ache of unworthiness anymore. There was another way, my brother. You did not kill yourself out of remorse for having lost Kathryn, but from having lost yourself.

Missing Pieces
Journal Exercises

RELATIONSHIPS: LOVE AND CHALLENGE

QUESTIONS FOR OTHERS

FINDING SUPPORTIVE CONNECTION

: Relationships have potential for both healing and distress. They may
provide safety, empathy, and the compassionate embrace of love, or
they may be a source of criticism, abuse, neglect, and betrayal. Write
in your journal about your loved one's experience in relationships, and
how they contributed to his instability or well-being:

: What were his dreams for love? What were his doubts and fears?

: How did his behavior and self-esteem change after getting
together with a partner? As the relationship progressed?

: What worked well for him in relationship? What brought pain
and suffering?

: During the times in your loved one's life when he experienced the
greatest life or emotional challenges, who stood by him? What
did they say or do that was supportive for him through difficult
times? What contributed to greater distress and dysfunction?

: How did he respond to relationship challenges? In what ways did
difficulties in his relationships contribute to his depression and
eventual suicide?

: Is there anyone you need or want to talk with about any of your loved
one's experiences shortly before the suicide? Contact that person,

explaining what you are interested in finding out and perhaps stating some of your specific questions. After your conversation, write a letter to your loved one, telling him what you learned and how you felt about it.

: Who do you turn to for comforting connection? Is there a way you might strengthen those connections? If you don't have them, how can you cultivate connection with others who can stand with you through your tragic loss and ongoing healing. A grief support group can be a good start. (See Appendix 2, "Creating Support." Also see Appendix 4, "Resources for Survivors of Suicide" that lists websites of organizations wth survivor's support groups in your area; and its subsection Resources for Creating Survivor Support Groups that offers guidance for creating and facilitating suicide bereavement support groups.)

Returning to the present moment . . .

Walk slowly around the room for a few minutes, recalling moments of kindness you have received, recently or even long ago.

I open my heart to the generosity of others.

17. Tracking the Unraveling

You are nine years old playing catch with your brother Gerry in the late autumn twilight in your backyard in Roxbury, a working class suburb of Boston. Your mom is calling out the window of your little two-story brick house on Sonoma Street.

"Larry! Gerry! Time for dinner!"

It's so dark you can hardly see, but you don't want to quit. "Just one more, Gerry. Throw me a pop-up. Come on Big Harps, way up there."

"Boys, I mean it! Now!" Her voice is shrill with insistence.

"Sure, Mom. We'll be right in," Gerry shouts. Then to you, little brother, "Okay, Little Harps, but this is it." And he launches the white baseball high into the afterglow of the evening sky. Up . . . up . . . up the spinning white hardball goes arching out over the patchy grass and weeds of the Harpel family's neglected backyard. In my mind, it falls into memories of the life you have just completed.

THEY SAY YOUR entire life passes before you at death. For Larry, that entire life, from childhood through his final days, was defined by his passion for baseball in general, and the Boston Red Sox in particular. *There were other passions as well, but baseball is the unifying theme that will guide this reflection back over your life, my brother.*

The white baseball comes down and is caught by your father, Aaron, a simple Jewish man. A shoe salesman. You looked up to your father and tried to emulate him. He was a good provider who genuinely cared about his wife and family. He was your first model of what a man should be. He was a quiet man. Soft-spoken and reserved, with a beautiful smile. You loved him deeply.

Sadly, we both shared the tragedy of losing our fathers when we were twenty. Larry was called home from college because his father had cancer. They took him to the hospital for a blood transfusion and, after the procedure, as Larry was pushing the wheelchair out the door, his father started yelling, "I can't see! I can't see!" As Larry vehemently described it to me, "Those bastards pumped the wrong blood into his veins and killed him!" *Your dad died in anger and blindness. Was that the moment you stopped trusting doctors?*

Fifteen years later, the Red Sox still hadn't won a World Series and Larry was in another hospital room in Los Angeles where his mother lay dying. Thinking she was still in Boston, she wanted to go home to the little house in Roxbury. *You told her there was no way to do that. She looked at you and simply shrugged. It was this last gesture that you often described. Your mother's shrug to life as if she were saying, "Oh well . . . ." Was it acceptance or giving up?*

—

The baseball hovers up there in the night sky and morphs into a big, white full moon over Boston, a reflection of the first of your three wives . . . Moon, who was Larry's hippie bride. Moon was Woodstock, smoking dope, hitchhiking, and living the long-haired life. *Man, you were a handsome cuss! You looked kind of like a Jewish Jessie Colin Young with your shoulder-length hair and black handlebar mustache. Moon was a barefoot Earth goddess. But when you came down from your '60s high, the Moon had set. She was gone.*

Next it was "Lynn-the-Liar" from Ohio. She was a one night stand, in a rainy suburb of Cleveland, that should never have gone any further. *You were on your way to California to become an actor. Lynn sent you perfumed letters, and there were long talks on the phone. Soon she visited you in Venice. She told you she was pregnant but that the baby wasn't yours. So you took her to Las Vegas, got married, and hitchhiked back to LA, riding most of the way in the bed of a pickup truck full of potatoes.* Two days later Lynn went back to Ohio. Turns out she wasn't pregnant. It was all a lie. When I asked Larry how long the marriage had lasted, he told me, "To give you an idea, on our first anniversary we both went out with different people."

—

It was 1990 and still no World Series win for the Red Sox at Fenway, but you hit a home run when you met Mary. She was the closest you had ever come at that point to true love. You had seven years of marriage with her, and you felt she was your friend, helpmate, and soul companion. You loved each other, supported each other through struggles. For a while it seemed good. I used to really admire the way you two worked on your relationship. You had couple's therapy before, during, and even after the marriage.

I wrote a country/rock song for their wedding, the last verse capturing what I saw and hoped for Larry:

> He's a family man in exile no more
> The family man in exile just opened the door
> I knew he'd be coming back again
> The family man in exile just got
> Married to . . . his best best friend.

When that marriage ended, there was no animosity, just your lingering disappointment and disillusionment with love.

———

The crowd cheers at the crack of the bat. Your eyes follow a high fly ball, and this time it lands in the mitt of an outfielder in Dodger Stadium under the hot southern California sun. Following every actor's dream to make it in TV or the movies, Larry headed to Hollywood. His dreams were realized when he landed a part on the 1980's television sitcom *Cheers* and became "Larry," one of the regulars sipping beers at that friendly Boston bar. It must have been almost like being back home.

There was a moment on the *Cheers* set that could have been a turning point, Larry's big break. The chief writer, Glen Charles, approached him one day for a little chitchat. "So tell me about the character you are when you're sitting at the bar," he asked. "What's this guy 'Larry' *really* like? Who is he?"

It was your moment. An actor's chance of a lifetime. You'd seen what the show did for Ted Danson and Kelsey Grammer—they got "discovered" and went on to their own fame. Now it seemed to be your turn. You looked at Glen Charles, and what you said next you regretted every day of your short acting career thereafter. You paused, scratched your bald head, and said, "Ah . . . hell, I don't know, man. You're the writer, you tell me."

If only he could have told Glen Charles who he, Larry Harpel, really was: a Red Sox fan, a lonely divorced guy down on his luck, a guy with a good heart who needed just one break. *But that's not what you said. Glen Charles walked away, and you never spoke to him again. The story you told yourself about your reply was that you had blown your chance. You condemned yourself and slunk away like a beaten dog with its tail between its legs.* So went Larry's confidence and his acting career. After *Cheers* the acting gigs were few and far between. *Maybe that wasn't the only way it had to go, Larry.*

———

You felt like you'd struck out in the last inning, but you dusted off your hurt pride, held your head high, and strode back up to the plate to take the next pitch. Larry always loved kids, and in his fortieth year he began to teach. That's when he really began to shine. Teaching became Larry's life.

For the first time in years you were happy. You had finally found your niche. Kids gravitated to you. They loved you. I've seen the magic you worked in the classroom with them. The walls were covered with their art and poetry that you inspired.

At the beginning of each school year, Larry sat his new students in a circle and passed a ball of red yarn from kid to kid until all were connected by a web of yarn. "This is a model of how our classroom will work," he told his students. "We are all interconnected." For that school year the "red web" would hang on the bulletin board. At the end of the year he took it down, cut the strands, and gave each child a piece of that connection to carry away.

You were fair to each student, settling disputes, nurturing everyone, and helping them develop their individual visions and talents. You always had time to address the problems and needs of each child. You were an exemplary teacher . . . honored by administrators, respected by parents, and held in the heart of every child.

When they heard about Larry's death, the folks at the school told the children he died in his sleep, and they wrote a tribute in their newsletter describing him as an "incredibly passionate teacher" who brought "that same fervor to his students. He was articulate and funny . . . his laugh infectious."

—

With the smell of fresh spring grass and the expectant squeals of boys all around, you reach into your bag of new baseballs and find the perfect one to toss out to the little pitcher standing on the mound. Larry coached a Little League baseball team for a couple of years with his brother Gerry. Of course, the team was the "Red Sox," and when they went zero and nineteen, somehow back then Larry was able to keep a bigger perspective. He inspired the team to use their defeats to build inner strength, courage, and determination, and to pour their hearts into the game even when the going was tough. *What happened to that strength, determination, and courage, Larry, when your going got tough? Where'd it go, my brother?*

A few years later, while kicking a soccer ball on a cement playground, Larry fell and shattered his right elbow, rendering his right arm useless. That's when the constant, unceasing pain began, and the nearly three-year break in teaching. There were doctor's appointments, pain blocks, countless x-rays, operations, and physical therapy. Still the shooting pain persisted day and night, and then began to radiate throughout his body. Nothing brought lasting relief. *That fall on the playground was the defining moment that precipitated your descent. You should have stayed with coaching baseball, Larry.*

Tracking the Unraveling
Journal Exercises

LIFE REVIEW

DEFINING MOMENTS

QUALITIES AND CONTRIBUTIONS

: Write a letter to your loved one reviewing her life. You might include scenes from childhood; relationships with parents, family, and friends; relationships with partners, lovers, and spouses; career aspirations, work, and livelihood; favorite activities; peak experiences and life-changing moments; values, beliefs, and spiritual or religious practices; goals and dreams; and more. Be creative. Step into her world and tell it from inside the life she lived. Bring her unique adventure alive.

: As you look back over your loved one's life, write a letter to her reflecting on what hurts, pains, disappointments, and "failures" may have triggered her downward spirals. What did she do to get through the losses and hardships of her life—both the wise and unwise choices? How were you affected by her actions? Was there a defining moment that precipitated her final descent?

: In what ways was your loved one valued and appreciated? Review her obituary, and talk with family members, friends, or colleagues who respected her qualities or contributions. Perhaps you can find written comments about her work or achievements. Write your own personal tribute in your journal.

Returning to the present moment . . .

Stand comfortably and gently shake out your body—wiggle your hands, shake
your arms, wiggle your feet, shake your legs.
Then close your eyes and breathe.

My spirit is light. My spirit is free.

18. Turning Point

It is August, ten months after Larry's suicide, and the Lost and Found Men's Council is gathering for its yearly retreat at Zaca Lake. This will be our first since Larry's death. When we arrive at the lodge, I walk out on the deck overlooking the beautiful green lake and surrounding mountains, the place where we'd all stood to take so many group pictures with Larry. Suddenly I'm struck by waves of sadness. Larry had been the one who urged us to begin coming here for our retreats. He'd loved Zaca with a passion, and being here makes the reality of his death painfully real. I feel the gnawing loneliness and emptiness that's all too familiar. I begin to let in how much I really miss him and how much I wish he were here. This year there are only four of us.

I rise early the next morning and decide to walk around the lake. There is still a thin white mist hovering over the surface of the water. I hear otherworldly squeals and yips of what I first think are dogs barking in the distance but I soon realize is a pack of coyotes. They screech and howl like devils or spirits from another dimension, then grow distant as they retreat up one of the nearby canyons.

As I wander, I find myself walking right to the spot where, three years earlier, Jeff, Larry, and I experienced the Chumash Bear Dance, a powerful Native American ritual we'd been invited to attend. I walk to the entrance of what had been the fire circle that night—a fifty-foot area that had been cleared and manicured down to the bare dirt. Now it is heavily overgrown with seed grass and weeds. I stand at the edge, next to a tree trunk pole with bear claws and other glyphs carved by the Chumash people. I recall the three of us watching the Chumash men in bearskins, dancing away the sorrows of the tribe before the blazing fire. I remember how we chanted and joined in the circle dance. Larry had taken the extra "sorrow turn" in the dance, putting his hands on the back of a Bear Dancer to purge himself of all the sorrow and pain he had endured for years from his injured arm and shoulder. I'd thought that his real healing had begun that night.

I touch the carved bear claw on the post, and immediately I have a sense of Larry's very real presence. If there were anywhere on earth that his spirit would want to inhabit, I realize it would be this spot by this beautiful pristine lake. After the Bear Dance that night, Larry even had the bear claw glyph tattooed on his shoulder. As I gaze across the circle, it occurs to me that perhaps his participation in that Chumash dance created an opening for his spirit to return and linger here. Whatever it is that I'm experiencing, I feel very close to Larry at this moment—like he's been holding this sacred space for me and the men of the Lost and Found. I cling to the spot. Can't leave.

Eventually I enter the ruins of the sacred circle. Tree stumps mark the Four Directions, and I sit for a while on each one, meditating and repeating a Buddhist chant about the impermanence of form. I feel like I'm going beyond ordinary consciousness—far beyond—to connect with Larry's spirit. As I move from tree stump to tree stump, I weep my sadness, missing my good friend, yet all the while continuing to feel his benevolent presence smiling on me. Larry seems to be welcoming me back to Zaca. I feel like he's silently telling me that it's alright. This forest, this wilderness, these rocks and this sacred lake are his home now, and everything is okay.

—

For my retreat activity, I'd planned for us to enact Samuel Beckett's play *Endgame* as a tribute to our departed friend. This four-character one-act play is about mortality and existential angst, which seems fitting. I want us to do the play as a ritual, in the most primitive shamanistic sense of theater-as-ceremony. It will be a way to evoke the spirit of Larry and to celebrate him. After all, our dear departed brother was an actor for a good part of his life.

The title of the play comes from chess, in which "endgame" refers to the final stages of a game when very few pieces remain, the stakes and tensions are high, and the last gambit is played to the ultimate checkmate. This play seems to be the perfect vehicle to go deeper into our feelings about losing our brother, who definitely played out his end-game. I think we might also use it to play out the endgame of our grief.

The play is essentially an end-of-life drama in which an ailing, decrepit character, Hamm, sits blindly in his wheelchair and spars verbally with Clov, his servant and only friend, on the meaninglessness of existence. Hamm asks Clov to use a telescope to look out the window to see what's happening in the outside world. All Clov ever sees is ruin and devastation. The seas are dead. And on land Clov sees that, "Nothing stirs. All is zero." For comic relief, Hamm listens to his parents conversing, each of them ensconced in their own garbage can. Great men's group material!

We make our way with our various props and costumes to the old abandoned geodesic dome that Larry, just this past summer, had dubbed the "Passion Dome," after he'd told us he was in love. We'd all danced our "Yes" to life there that night. By the time we arrive there now, it's pitch dark, but I have flashlights for everyone to read by. I've cast myself as Hamm, and I wear a toque and sunglasses since the character is blind. As stated in the stage directions, I hang a whistle on a cord around my neck to summon Clov. I've provided the appropriate props for the others as well. For Jeff, who plays Clov, a toy telescope, flea powder, an alarm clock, and a three-legged stuffed dog. For Cory, who is playing Nagg, the father, there is a white old man's beard and a nightcap, and a white granny bonnet for Bruce, who's playing Nell, Hamm's mother.

The brothers rise to the occasion, getting completely into their roles. The upshot of this experience is that reading this play, and viewing it through the lens of our experience with Larry's suicide, is giving both the play and Larry's death a new relevance. For me, there is a particular moment that illuminates and transforms my feelings about Larry's suicide. At the end of an exchange between Clov and Hamm, Clov says:

> I say to myself—sometimes, Clov, you must learn to suffer better than that if you want them to weary of punishing you—one day. I say to myself—sometimes, Clov, you must be better than that if you want them to let you go—one day. But I feel too old, and too far, to form new habits. Good, it'll never end, I'll never go. (Pause.)

Then one day, suddenly, it ends, it changes, I don't under-
stand, it dies, or it's me, I don't understand that either. I ask the
words that remain—sleeping, waking, morning, evening.
They have nothing to say.
(*Pause.*)
I open the door of the cell and go.

These last words spoken by Clov turn it all around for me. I see that
Larry's life had become his own private prison. A jail of his own making.
He was incarcerated inside his depression and pain, and he saw the act of
suicide as his only exit, his only way out of his intractable imprisonment.
Larry opened the door to his cell and simply left.

—

The realization brought on by Clov's line changed me. After all these
months, my own pain and resistance are falling away, and I am finally
beginning to accept what Larry had done. When I returned home from
Zaca Lake, I found myself looking in a new way at the pictures of Larry I'd
put up in my writing room. I realized I'd been avoiding really looking at
his photos for months because of my anger and inability to forgive him.
I was finally able to make eye contact again with Larry in those images.

We are all different after the retreat. Returning to Zaca and performing that play in the Passion Dome helped us to pay homage to our fallen
brother, helped us begin to move beyond our grief, and helped us to
embrace Larry and ourselves in forgiveness and acceptance. We love
him and always will. But now the journey is about us and our continuing
struggles and joys, conflicts and triumphs, successes and failures as men.
At last we have begun to heal. Now we are truly the "Lost *and* Found."
Before we left Zaca we'd taken a new group picture on the deck overlooking the lake. I keep that photo on my bulletin board—it's entitled "And
then we were four."

—

It has taken almost a year, but we're beginning to see the hidden gifts of
Larry's death for each of us. At our Lost and Found meeting in September,
a month before the first anniversary of his suicide, we share the amazing

realizations we're all having. We're seeing that Larry's death has been an unanswered question that each of us is now beginning to answer in his own way.

Jeff is beginning to discover emotions and feelings that, because of the dominance of his rational mind, have been shut down in him for most of his life. Now he is entering territory he probably never would have gotten to had it not been for the shock of Larry's untimely departure. Cory, who always played the quiet "kid brother" role to Larry's "big brother" persona, tells us that Larry's death somehow has encouraged him to be more himself. He is now consciously living his life to develop some of what he considers the best qualities Larry embodied: outspokenness, boldness, and risk-taking. Bruce is exploring aspects of grief that have been buried since the death of his sister.

For me, Larry's final gift was the impetus to explore all my mixed emotions brought on by his suicide and to write this book, my attempt to complete our conversation, and then to offer my journey as an avenue to healing for others. Although I now realize that my conversation with Larry will always remain unfinished, exploring my grief sustained and strengthened me as I recovered from the tragedy. I have also begun to open to the healing and unimpeded love that comes with forgiveness.

It has taken nearly a year, but the men of the Lost and Found are finally able to accept our brother's suicide as a question that each of us will continue to answer—a question that forces us to confront certain eternal truths about our personal and spiritual values and our own mortality. And we're beginning to see and feel Larry's untimely exit as a bequest to each of us . . . a final parting gift. In his dying, Larry offered us an opportunity to grow, to put things in perspective, and to come to a fuller understanding of life. His passing challenged each of us to ask vital questions about love, who we are as men, the meaning of brotherhood, forgiveness, and what it means to be alive.

Turning Point
Journal Exercises

THE HEALING STORY

THE POWER OF PLACE

GIFTS AND LESSONS

TURNING TOWARD ACCEPTANCE

: Find a piece of literature—a story, film, or play—that you feel relates to your loved one. Read or view it, trusting that it holds a key to your healing. Write about what gets stirred in you and how it may cast a new light on your understanding of your loved one and his suicide.

: If possible, return to a place that held positive meaning for your loved one. You may want to create your own spontaneous ritual of mourning there.

: Write a letter to your loved one describing the hidden gifts that have been revealed through his suicide. Tell him what growth, change, or connection with yourself and others have emerged.

: Write to your loved one about any turning points toward acceptance and forgiveness you may have experienced in your grieving process. Describe the time, the setting, and what the circumstances were that enabled you to transform the grief.

Returning to the present moment . . .

Bring to mind someone you love who may be hurting.
Place your hand on your heart and breathe out compassion.

May your pain and sorrow ease. May you be at peace.

19. Discovering Interbeing

October 15, 2006: Larry, today is exactly one year since you took your own life. My feelings and relationship with you have begun to change and evolve with the passage of time. It now seems to me that it is an extremely limited concept to think of "being" as restricted to our physical bodies. Zen Master Thich Nhat Hanh uses the word "interbeing" to describe the interconnectedness of us all. Our words, acts, and interactions with others exist in our minds and memories as we continue to inter-be with everyone we have ever known or had contact with. They're a part of us and we're a part of them. For myself, what I've come to know is that if I look with that deeper understanding, then every word, every feeling, every memory connected with you is still a part of me and all those who knew and loved you.

Larry still exists within each of the men of the Lost and Found. We are his continuation. So in a very real sense Larry is alive in each of us. And by healing ourselves, we begin to heal those parts of Larry that exist within us. We open to receive the gifts he has given that forever changed us and that inform the paths we each must now travel without him.

Larry and I meant so much to each other, and I am realizing that nothing, not even death, can take that away. Rather than ending with his death, my relationship with Larry is continuing to unfold. As time passes I can increasingly recall our shared experiences with appreciation and affection.

On the Fourth of July, this first summer after Larry's death, I take Buddy and Dizzy out for a walk. When I pull out the fold-up water dish that Larry always brought with us on our walks, I feel a sudden sense of gratitude. Later I mention it in one of the many letters that I continue to write to my departed friend.

The dogs were frightened by the pop and fizzle of the firecrackers that were going off all day today. But at the end of our walk they became peaceful, their tongues long and wet from slurping water that I poured into the canvas water dish you had given me, my dear friend. The dogs' wet tongues also remember you and your kindness on those hot days we all walked together. You never forgot to bring bottles of water that you poured gurgling into that green canvas for their parched throats. Their lapping tongues remind me that such a friendship as ours never lacked for the water which, even now after all this time, still quenches the deepest thirst.

As I find the courage to continue the journey through the peaks and valleys of my grieving and healing process, I sometimes find myself coming to rest on the shores of a release, a soft relief in my heart that I have come to recognize as forgiveness. But even with this growing surrender, I still go through waves of outrage, deep currents of hurt and sorrow, lingering guilt and shame, and periods of fear and confusion.

In one of my journal dialogues with Larry, I start again with anger, swearing, recriminations, and blame . . . and then suddenly the conversation turns. After a poignant pause, Larry's response begins coming out in a different and unexpected tone.

"Listen, Bob . . . hell, can't we just put all this behind us. We don't see or speak to each other all that much any more these days, and I hate to fight like this when we have this rare opportunity. Hey, I love you man . . . my brother— my teacher."

"I remember that's what you used to call me."

"And I meant it. Man, you helped me discover so much."

"Nah . . . it wasn't me, Lar. That stuff was already there inside you. We discovered a lot of it together."

"Well, yeah . . . maybe. I know you're right, but you helped me understand myself better. Take the compliment, Bob."

"Okay. Thanks, Lar."

As I finish writing, I feel a great weight lifting from my heart. I am beginning to let go of the suffering I have been carrying for so long from the past, and I sense the first glimmers of forgiveness for Larry—and for myself. I can feel the pain and the price of keeping my heart closed to this man I so loved. I let these feelings carry over into my writing as I continue . . . *For now I can summon only a whisper, my brother . . . I forgive you. I know that what you did that caused me pain came from your own anger, your confusion, and your fear. While I don't agree with your choices, I can feel in my heart forgiveness for your pain and suffering, and the actions that arose from them. I forgive you. And I want you to know that whatever you did in the past, however you caused me anguish, it's time for me to welcome you back into my heart.*

Eventually I come to recognize that to truly heal, I also need to directly ask for Larry's forgiveness. *Larry, my friend, for all the ways I may have caused you pain through my judgment, outrage, hurt, and confusion, for all the ways I acted or failed to act, I ask for your forgiveness. For all the ways I pushed you out of my heart and made you wrong and bad, for all the ways I judged and was critical of you, I ask you now to forgive me. Please my brother, forgive me.*

And I need to forgive myself as well, for all of the shame, self-judgment, and reactive anger; for the ways I have abandoned and not cared for myself; and for the relentless critical self-talk and guilt that has plagued me since Larry's death. In order to truly heal, I have to be willing to let all that go and welcome myself back into my own heart, as if welcoming home a guest who has been away for too long. I need to say, "I forgive you," to myself.

With patience and the courage of compassion, I am gradually learning to open beyond the pain and all the ways my mind and heart have wanted to contract. Something deep inside has softened and sighed, as if I can finally take a full breath again.

I know that my healing also requires that I finally say good-bye to the Larry I knew when he was alive; good-bye to all the good times I had with him; to any of the difficulties we had in our friendship; and to the dreams that will never come true with him. I have to let him go.

What I'm discovering is that the more I release him, the more I can connect with an affection and love for Larry that transcends his form. I can begin to smile when I think about my friend and the many wonderful experiences we shared through the years. With letting go and forgiveness also comes acceptance. I accept that we had an amazing friendship and that, all things being impermanent, it had run its course. And I also see that the truths we shared as friends and as men will always be accessible to me. The realization of my interbeing with Larry is helping me to move beyond the pain and feel a true enduring connection with him. I thank the universe that I had the honor of knowing Larry and sharing the brief moment that had been our fifteen-year friendship. I also accept that he is gone.

I can now say good-bye to you, my brother, knowing that you will forever be a part of me. I bid you farewell, Larry. Whatever blocks my heart and the freedom of yours, I choose to let that all go. May we both be free from suffering. May we connect through the peace that we both long for. May you go in peace, my brother. May you go in peace.

Discovering Interbeing
Journal Exercises

LIVING ON INSIDE YOU

FORGIVENESS

THE GOOD-BYE LETTER

: How do you experience "interbeing" with your loved one? How does she continue to live in you and those who loved her?

: It takes great courage to open your heart in forgiveness of your loved one, and of yourself. Let the *possibility* of forgiveness enter your heart, and when you feel ready, try the following, either silently to yourself or by writing in your journal:

   : Offer forgiveness to your loved one for the ways she knowingly or unknowingly through the years hurt you by her anger, fear, pain, confusion, actions, or inaction. "I forgive you for . . ."

   : Ask for forgiveness of your loved one for the ways that you have knowingly or unknowingly hurt her by your own anger, fear, pain, confusion, actions, or inaction. "I ask for your forgiveness for . . ."

   : Offer forgiveness to yourself for ways that you have knowingly or unknowingly caused harm to yourself through your own anger, fear, pain, confusion, actions, or inaction. "I forgive myself for . . ."

Forgiveness is an ongoing practice that can't be rushed. Tragic loss and great grief take time to heal and integrate into a larger perspective of life. Simply let your heart meet the pain, again and again, with patience, kindness, and compassion.*

: When you feel ready, write a good-bye letter to your loved one:

> : Say good-bye to what you enjoyed with her and your relationship with her.
>
> : Say good-bye to what was difficult or painful between you throughout your relationship.
>
> : Say good-bye to the dreams that will never come true with her.
>
> : Close with, "What I really want you to know is . . ." and share with her how you are now holding her life and death with more perspective and meaning.

Returning to the present moment . . .

Place your hand on your heart and breathe gently.

I love you. Good-bye.
I love you. Good-bye.

---

*Adapted from Jack Kornfield, *The Wise Heart: A Guide to the Universal Teachings of Buddhist Psychology* (New York, NY: Bantam Books, 2009).

EPILOGUE

SAYING GOOD-BYE TO MY BUDDY

There's no easy way for me to break this to you, Larry. Buddy has a tumor. Actually, this is his third tumor. The first two were in his left elbow. The vet did a masterful job performing two operations, but it was impossible to get all of it. He warned that this is a very aggressive type of cancer and that the elbow is a very difficult place to heal.

Elbow . . . does that sound familiar, Larry? How ironic! You and your beloved bear of a dog are bedeviled by wounded elbows. Every time I bandage his left elbow—the sore that will not heal—I think of your sore elbow that led you into the cancer of your depression. Doc Jones gives Buddy less than a year with this third tumor just having sprouted on his shoulder—yes, another area of pain you two have in common.

—

BUDDY WAS WITH ME for almost three years after Larry's death. In his own dying process, Buddy gave me the opportunity I never had with Larry—the opportunity to face his death, to tell him how much I loved him, to say good-bye, and to help him die with dignity and compassion. Buddy's dying and death was an unexpected gift, a vital part of my grief and healing journey.

When I took Buddy on as my own dog, I began to see that he was an ally and guide for me, helping me through my period of grief and reconciliation after Larry's suicide. Buddy was a link with Larry that continued on, and he taught me a lot about the fortitude that is necessary to continue through hard times. Buddy embodied solidity and determination. As a Husky, he was bred to be one of a team, pulling a sled through snow and slush, and his role in my healing was to pull the sled of my grief through that long period of healing.

With dogged determination, he was there no matter what, with unwavering loyalty and joy. Yes, joy! Buddy was a perpetually happy dog, even in the face of death—both his own and Larry's. He seemed to take it all in stride with great courage. His wagging tail, smiling jowls, and woofing comments on life saw me through the darkest hours after Larry's death. And in his remaining days, I had the opportunity to provide love, healing, and comfort for him, as he had for me.

Each precious day as I bandaged his elbow, I looked into his big brown eyes, told him I loved him, and said good-bye again and again. I fed him and supplied him with whatever healing balms or salves I could find. I removed whatever sources of pain I could, and beamed health and love to him. I provided comfort and peace. I greeted him with gratitude each morning and said a final farewell to him each night.

One Sunday, during the meditation period at Agape Spiritual Center, I chose to hold Buddy in my heart and radiate love and compassion to him. I embraced him as a manifestation of the loving Spirit of the universe, with a cold nose and a wagging tail. As I reflected in the sacred silence, I had a very comforting vision of Buddy coming into existence, being birthed, and romping with a litter of seven little fur balls. I saw him develop from that pup into a strapping young dog, a powerful dog. I saw him with his first master who treated him harshly, abused and abandoned him. I saw him in the rescue shelter being found by Larry, who gave Buddy abundant attention, friendship, and love. Larry's sensitive care undid the former abuse, and for about seven years Bud had a loving home. I saw Buddy by Larry's side through his master's untimely departure. I saw him become *my* buddy. And I saw him completing his life's journey.

Our furry friend is approaching death, Larry, and his teaching and healing roles are nearing an end. Soon I must resolve to go it alone. Buddy is moving on.

I knew there would come a point when I couldn't allow the little guy to suffer anymore and could no longer justify ongoing treatment to keep him alive. I constantly asked myself by what authority do we humans have the right to determine when a dog's life should be ended. I also became acutely aware of the irony of this situation with regard to my friend's suicide. If I can choose to release my dog from life because I feel that he is suffering acutely, then why not allow for the suicide of a person like Larry who chooses to release himself due to the intensity of suffering that made him feel he could no longer remain alive? These are questions of such magnitude, depth, and far-reaching consequence, they will continue to be grappled with by poets and mystics, belief systems and political systems, for as long as there is life, death, and free will.

I continue to wrestle with the depth of my responsibility in making this life and death decision, Larry. Every decision I make regarding Buddy is my decision alone . . . but it's also yours, my dear friend. What would you do, I keep wondering. Weighing the gravity of these decisions, I am beginning to see that some of my conflicted uncertainty may come from the realization that letting go of Buddy will also be another level of letting go of you.

———

Tuesday, August 12, 2008: Buddy left us today. It was a gentle farewell. This morning he was asleep in the kitchen by his water bowl in exactly the same position he'd been the night before. I made him breakfast, which he barely touched. When I called him to get up and go outside, he tried to stand on his own but could not. That's when I really knew that the end was here. The choice was now clear and I made that definitive phone call. Dr. Valentine was able to come over at 2:30 for a home euthanasia.

I lit some sage and placed bouquets of flowers on either side of his blanket on the back porch. All the while I was playing a recorded chant for the sick and dying by His Holiness the Dalai Lama. It continued throughout that afternoon as a sacred backdrop.

Tenderly, I carried Buddy outside and laid him on the blanket. The sage smoke kept the flies away from the open wound on his leg. I set up a small altar with a candle and flowers, a photo of Larry and Buddy, and a picture of Amitabha, the Buddha of boundless life and infinite light. An unexpected midafternoon breeze flickered the candle flame—was it Larry's spirit-wind coming for Buddy? I used the eagle wing of the Lost and Found to waft the sage smoke over Buddy and the ritual space. He remained peaceful through it all.

I gave him some water to drink a couple of times. Spoke to him. Releasing him. Telling him it was okay to leave. Telling him I was letting him go.

I read poems to him and chanted *Om mani padme hum*. It is believed in Tibetan Buddhism that this chant, if heard by a dying animal, is supposed to give him the opportunity of human rebirth in his next incarnation. Buddy had certainly earned it.

Lost and Found brother Bruce arrived at 2 p.m. He brought his drum, and we drummed slowly and softly to the chanting of His Holiness. Dizzy's bark signaled the arrival of Dr. Valentine, and he and Amy joined us on the back porch. All the while Buddy lay peacefully, stirring for moments as if he wanted to get up, then settling back down again. Dr. V examined and listened deeply to him, and affirmed that Buddy was ready to leave. Amy began to tearfully read a poem I had written, "I Will Take Care of Your Dog Buddy":

> When someone dies—man or dog—it's a terrible thing.
> It's something to take note of,
> It's something to sit silently with,
> It's something to cry about and wonder about and cry about,
> Because life is so damn precious and . . .
> Yes, I said I would take care of your dog.

I stroked his soft fur and felt the silence of the garden. I began reading the words from Rabindranath Tagore's "Peace, My Heart," as Dr. V gave Buddy his first tranquilizer shot.

> Let the time for parting be sweet.
> Let it not be a death, but completeness.
> Let love melt into memory
> And pain into songs.

Bud became even more peaceful . . .

> Stand still, oh beautiful end,
> For a moment,
> And say your last words in silence . . .

I held his head and continued to chant *Om mani padme hum*.

Space and time opened up. Countless moments passed, and then the soft cooing of a distant dove beckoned through the silence. I signaled Dr. V that it was time for the final injection. I held Buddy's head, looking lovingly into his eyes while I continued to chant. I really couldn't tell when he stopped breathing. There was no decisive moment when I knew he was gone. Nothing changed in our connection as he silently slipped away. He just seemed to be peacefully sleeping. I held his head for a long time. His body remained warm. When Dr. V listened with his stethoscope, he found no heartbeat. I stroked the thick rich black fur on Buddy's back, running my fingers through it for the last time. And then I let him go, the last lines of Tagore's poem echoing in my mind . . .

> I bow to you and hold up my lamp
> To light you on your way.

It was a very peaceful end. A quiet ending. A release. Buddy is free. And I too feel somehow freer. Lighter.

I am writing these words high in the hills overlooking the blue Pacific near the City of Angels that was home to Buddy and Larry. I have brought my memories to scatter to the winds.

A soft summer breeze blows by like spirit smoke. I bow. *Good-bye, Buddy. Thank you, Buddy. I love you, Buddy. Good-bye, Larry. Thank you, Larry. I love you, Larry. Your dog has given me the opportunity to truly say good-bye . . . and to let go.*

In Memory of
Larry Harpel 1950–2005   Buddy Budster 1994–2008

Saying Good-bye to My Buddy
Journal Exercises

The Gift of Grieving Again

Recreating the Final Hours

Ongoing Conversation

Paying It Forward

Reclaiming Your Life

: Like my experience with Buddy, there may be an event months or even years after the death of your loved one that allows you to grieve and say good-bye at deeper and deeper levels. If you've had such an experience, write about it in your journal.

: One aspect of healing is completing in the present what was not able to be completed in the past. Sit quietly and contemplate the way you would have wanted to care for your loved one had he died naturally. In your journal write to him what you would have wanted to say and do through the course of his dying and death. Write the dialogue that you would have wanted to share in those final hours and moments together . . . and after. Do now what you weren't able to do then.

: As the years go by after the loss of your loved one, allow the conversation to continue. How are you changing as a result of the suicide. Emotionally? Spiritually? What has your loved one's suicide moved you to explore more fully in your own life? Create new dialogues when you feel called to do so, acknowledging the enduring connection you share. Add thoughts, memories, stories, and creative expressions to your journal as they arise. Just as your conversation with your loved one will always remain open, your journey of letting go and healing from such a great loss will continue to unfold.

: The memory of Larry and the healing that took place in me after his suicide allowed me to sow the seeds of my transformation in the form of this book. Envision ways that you can allow the memory of your loved one to be a seed to grow something of meaning or beauty for others, then cultivate these seeds and let them begin to take root.

: As you continue to heal, consider opening your heart to others who have suffered a similar loss or are in the pain of grief. Bring to mind someone close to you who's hurting and who you'd be willing to reach out to and support. Find ways of broadening your compassion to serve others in your community who would appreciate your care. Consider making a phone call to someone in need, gathering together or joining a support group of survivors, or volunteering for a local hospice or service agency. What steps might you make to reach out?

: A final step of healing from such great loss is to begin to reclaim your life by creating the conditions for more well-being. Journal about what thoughts and feelings arise as you consider living more fully and enjoying your life. What simple things could you do each day to invite more relaxation, pleasure, or fulfillment? Consider ways to spend time with friends or family to enjoy more closeness and connection and fun. Notice what happens when you incline your mind toward more contentment and happiness.

Returning to the present moment . . .

Sit with your hands resting on your lap, palms up.
Feel a smile rise inside you. As you inhale, open your heart to
the fullness of life. As you exhale, send out blessings.

May I love and live fully.

Appendices

Appendix 1

Tool Kit for Your Journey to Healing

Marilynne Chöphel MFT
(A printable version of the "Tool Kit" is available at
www.unfinishedconversation.com)

As you embark on your grief and healing journey, it's important that
you have the tools to help you move through the challenges and changes
you will inevitably face. This Tool Kit is a guide to help you make choices
that will help you create more stability and well-being in your life, even
in the midst of your grief.

 **Travel Advisory** Always carry a supportive Tool Kit and travel with trusted companions. Proceed with compassion and remember to take along the basics:

▶ Mindful Observation
▶ Supportive Resources
▶ Fellow Travelers and Guides
▶ Emotional Weather Barometer
▶ Map of the Territory of Grief
▶ Inner Compass
▶ Instructions for Meditation: Sitting and Walking
▶ Tonglen Meditation: Taking in Pain and Sending Out Relief

Mindful Observation

Perhaps the most important tool for navigating your entire journey is being mindful—simply paying attention, without judgment, to
whatever you are experiencing inside and around you. No matter what is
happening at any moment, you can find a calm place inside that observes

what is there without being caught up in it or overwhelmed by it. Like taking a walk through a forest and noticing the trees, you can notice your experience moment to moment. Especially when you're going through a difficult time, letting yourself be aware of the following aspects of your experience can help you get some relief and perspective.

Notice these five primary ways of organizing experience and add your own ideas:

▸ **Thoughts:** Memories of the past, imaginings of the future, beliefs, values, "shoulds," judgments, self-limiting thoughts, cognitive distortions, intentions, aspirations, the "story" you tell yourself about yourself, others, and life.

▸ **Emotions:** Anger/outrage, fear/anxiety, surprise, sadness/despair, shame/disgust, hurt/anguish, vulnerability, mood swings, overwhelm, kindness/compassion, gratitude/forgiveness, joy/peace, affection/love.

▸ **Five Senses:** Smelling, tasting, seeing, hearing, touching/physical sensation.

▸ **Movement:** Pushing, reaching, walking, collapsing/lengthening, kicking, throwing, punching, jerking, shaking, clenching, contracting/expanding, frowning/smiling, crying/laughing, freezing, taking action.

▸ **Inner Body Sensations:** Agitation/calm, pain/pleasure, heavy/light, open/closed, supported/collapsed, tense/relaxed, strong/weak, tingling, vibrating, pulsing, trembling, numb, short and shallow breathing/full and relaxed breathing.

As you journey through this book, listen in on these five levels and meet your experience with an attitude of curiosity, exploration, and kindness. Practice remaining aware of your experience, just as it is, without judgment and with compassion, even when it is difficult. Remember there's no right or wrong way to feel—simply observe what you are experiencing and, when you are ready, express it in your journal or with someone you trust.

Supportive Resources

The greater the impact of your tragic loss and distress, the more resources you need to balance their effect. To survive the aftermath of your heartbreaking loss and move forward on your journey of healing, you will need to develop both internal and external supports.

What Are Your Inner Supports?

Turn inward to connect with these inner realms. Be creative and add your own ideas:

- ▶ **Your Psychological Life:** Self-awareness, choice, stability, patience, courage, empathy, compassion, forgiveness, determination, wise choices, creating safety and comfort for yourself, ability to be flexible, adaptive, curious, and open.

- ▶ **Your Relationships with Others:** Ability to connect with friends, family, and strangers, communication skills, capacity to give and receive support, healthy boundaries, capacity for and cultivation of empathy and compassion, capacity to be vulnerable and intimate, capacity to give and receive affection and love.

- ▶ **Your Spiritual Life:** Faith, inspiration, devotion, connection with something greater than yourself, prayer, meditation, capacity for and cultivation of harmony, mercy, tranquility, equanimity, surrender, reverence, wonder, happiness and joy, pure awareness.

- ▶ **Your Emotional Life:** Ability to feel and accept a full range of emotions from joy to sorrow, recognizing changes in your emotions, ability to regulate your emotions when alone or with others, experiencing life's challenges without flooding with emotion or shutting down, being able to think and feel at the same time.

- ▶ **Your Intellectual Life:** Capacity to reflect, think things through, solve problems, develop perspective, learn new things, imagination, reasoning, integrity, perseverance, motivation, interest, open-minded inquiry.

- ▸ **Your Body:** Self-care, supporting your health, relaxation, deep sleep, moderation, ability to laugh and cry, capacity to enjoy the pleasures of the five senses..

- ▸ **Your Creative Life:** Journaling, expressing yourself through art, singing, playing music, writing, poetry, dancing, visioning, creating what has meaning.

- ▸ **Your Natural World:** Ability to appreciate beauty and nature, relationship with animals, ability to play and have fun.

What Are Your Outer Supports?

Reach out to connect with these outer realms. Be creative and add your own ideas:

- ▸ **relationships:** Friends, family, children, coworkers, social and recreational groups; skillful and caring communication; nurturing relationships with friends, family, and colleagues; generosity; giving support and service; enjoyment of interpersonal connection and intimacy.

- ▸ **Community:** Group connection, sharing meals and other activities, parties and celebrations, shared sports and recreation, shared holidays and rituals, support groups, health care providers, therapists, classes and workshops, continuing education, social service agencies, volunteering and serving others.

- ▸ **Your Material World:** Creating safety and stability in your home, finances, and relationships.

- ▸ **Your Spiritual World:** Spiritual practices and study, meditating or praying with others, spiritual community, ritual.

- ▸ **Your Intellectual World:** Reading, learning, continuing education, dialogue and debate, intellectual stimulation, games/puzzles, lectures and performances, scientific curiosity, new experiences, culture, and travel.

- **Your Healthy Body:** Good nutrition, exercising to develop strength and flexibility, deep relaxation, sports, body-mind practices such as yoga or Qigong, martial arts.

- **Creative Nourishment:** Writing, poetry, art, music, singing, photography, dancing, listening to music, reading, cultural activities, performances, classes, creative projects.

- **Your Natural World:** Spending time in nature, gardening, animal companions, travel and learning about different cultures, scientific curiosity and learning, exploration and adventure.

FELLOW TRAVELERS AND GUIDES

A feeling of disconnection from not just your loved one, but also from those around you and from yourself, is natural after such sudden and tragic loss. Sharing your experience with someone who truly understands your grief is an important part of resolving the loss and healing. (See Appendix 2, "Creating Support") Optimally your network of support will include:

- **Your People:** Talk individually or gather with friends, family members, or others whom you trust to understand and care.

- **Journey Buddy:** Meet regularly with someone you trust, perhaps another survivor, who listens well, truly understands, and supports your healing.

- **Support Group:** Come together with others in a survivor's support group or grief support group. (See Appendix 4, "Resources for Survivors of Suicide" for websites of organizations with survivor's support groups, and its subsection Resources for Creating Survivor Support Groups that offers guidance for creating and facilitating suicide bereavement support groups.)

- **Travel Guide:** Work with a licensed therapist, grief counselor, mental health or health care professional, or spiritual counselor. If it's possible for you to work with a therapist, select someone who is licensed, experienced, and has had some training in the treatment of traumatic experience. It's important that you work with someone you feel safe and comfortable with. Most therapists will offer an initial brief session for you to meet and interview them. There are many different approaches to therapy. We would suggest finding a method that works with how your loss has affected you mentally, emotionally, as well as the effects on your body and nervous system. The following are organizations of therapists who use such holistic approaches, are highly respected in the professional therapeutic community, and have websites that list licensed therapists near you.

- Sensorimotor Psychotherapy Institute
  www.sensorimotorpsychotherapy.org

- EMDR Institute
  www.emdr.com

- Foundation for Human Enrichment
  www.traumahealing.com

- Emotionally Focused Therapy for Couples
  www.iceeft.com

EMOTIONAL WEATHER BAROMETER

Pause occasionally during your reading, writing, or sharing to become aware of your present-moment experience. Distress triggers the fight-flight-freeze responses of the nervous system. You might feel agitated and full of anger at one moment, anxious and afraid the next, and later find yourself feeling passive and disconnected.

Remember that your intention is to heal, not to re-traumatize. If you find yourself beginning to feel hijacked by intense emotions, stuck in avoidance, or overwhelmed by memories, step back from what you are focusing on until you feel more stable again. Return awareness to your body and breath, re-connect with what is grounding and comforting in

APPENDIX 1 : 139

the present moment, and turn to your Supportive Resources and caring connections for comfort.

In order to transform and heal through your grief, it's important to learn how to navigate through strong feelings and stressful situations without being overwhelmed by the emotion or shutting down and going numb. Explore ways to engage with the exercises in bite-size-pieces so that you stay within your "window of tolerance," choosing an emotional range and pace for yourself that feels safe, containable, and where you can bring compassionate awareness and choice to your exploration of thoughts, feelings, and physical sensations. Remember that as the suffering of the past is met with the caring connection, wise perspective, and accepting embrace of the present, the traces of pain can arise, transform, and heal.

Whenever distressing feelings surface, think of them as passing weather systems—they will change—and simply notice your experience. You may sometimes feel *hyperaroused*: flooded by emotions, agitated, anxious, overwhelmed, dealing with racing thoughts, panicked, self-conscious, defensive and reactive, needing to control everything, or unable to stop crying. You may also sometimes feel *hypoaroused*: barely able to feel emotions, frozen and numb, passive, paralyzed, unable to think straight, shut down, disconnected from your self, immobilized, apathetic and uncaring, disorganized, or unable to cry.

Pushing away your feelings will only bury them, so allow emotions, whatever they are, to arise and pass through you in a way that feels manageable. Notice if you want to express what you're feeling in writing, through action, or by talking with someone, but also know that feeling something doesn't necessarily mean you have to act on it.

Practice meeting difficult emotions, thoughts, memories, or conditions with the four steps of "RAIN," a mindfulness-based technique from meditation teacher Michele McDonald, to transform them into more manageable experience from which wise choices and skillful action becomes possible.

R — Recognize what is happening inside and around you with compassionate awareness. Notice the thoughts, emotions, and physical sensations so that they can be acknowledged and responded to. "I am having this thought right now." "Sadness is present."

A — Allow your experience to be present. Accept the thoughts, emotions, and physical sensations to be as they are in this moment, without resisting or holding on. Notice as they arise, change, and pass away. "Let it be." "I receive this moment as it is."

I — Investigate your experience with curiosity, openness, and a natural desire to know the truth of your own experience and that of others. Study the thoughts, emotions, and physical sensations with an attitude of kindness and compassion. "What physical sensations am I feeling?" "What emotions are present?" "What is the story I am telling myself?"

N — Non-identification allows for meeting your experience with a spacious, neutral awareness and an open heart. These thoughts, feelings, and physical sensations are not unique to you, but are experienced by all people. "Rest in a compassionate open awareness that holds even this."

You can also choose calming and soothing activities such as gentle breathing, taking a break to stretch, or taking a walk. Or simply recall something beautiful and nourishing in your life, a moment of kindness you received, or something or someone you are grateful for. Remember to draw upon your Inner and Outer Supports to help you stay safe and balanced as you move through your grief and create more stability and well-being.

> When you contact the all-worked-up feeling of shenpa (getting hooked on a negative emotion), the basic instruction is the same as in dealing with physical pain. Whether it's a feeling of I like or I don't like, or an emotional state like loneliness, depression, or anxiety, you open yourself fully to the sensation, free of interpretation. If you've tried this approach with physical pain, you know that the

result can be quite miraculous. When you give your full attention to
your knee or your back or your head—whatever hurts—and drop
the good/bad, right/wrong story line and simply experience the
pain directly for even a short time, then your ideas about the pain,
and often the pain itself, will dissolve.

—Pema Chödrön*

MAP OF THE TERRITORY OF GRIEF

Losing someone to suicide is traumatizing, and the bereavement is complex. It's important to remember that the responses to loss are unique to each person, and all are quite normal reactions to an event as life altering as losing someone you love to suicide.

Dr. Elisabeth Kübler-Ross described five different experiences that commonly take place during any grieving process. They are not sequential, and they may occur separately or simultaneously. They may vary in intensity, change by the hour, or persist for days, months, or even longer. Feel free to add to these categories from your own personal experience of grief.

- ▶ **Denial:** You try to minimize, ignore, or refuse to accept your feelings, and/or the reality of the situation and its impact on you. "This can't be happening." "I feel fine." "It's not that bad."

- ▶ **Anger:** This can be turned outward against others with irritability, impatience, criticism, frustration, blame, contempt, withdrawal of attention/affection, passive-aggressive behaviors, outbursts, outrage, aggression. Or it can be turned inward against yourself in self-judgment, self-blame, shame, withdrawal, self-destructive behaviors, self-harm. "It's not fair!" "Why me?!" "How could I let this happen?!" "Who's to blame?"

- ▶ **Bargaining:** You try to negotiate with reality by focusing on all of the "if-onlys." "If only *that* did or didn't happen." "If only he or I

*Pema Chödrön, *Living Beautifully: with Uncertainty and Change* (Boston, MA: Shambhala Publications, 2012).

did or didn't, say or do, *that*." "If only *this* had happened before or after *that*."

▸ Depression: You experience deep sadness and feel depressed most of the day. You may feel fatigued and want to stay in bed all day, or you may be unable to sleep. You may overeat or have no appetite. You may feel helpless, hopeless, or have diminished interest or pleasure in activities. You may feel irritable, anxious, and agitated, or feel shut down and immobilized. You may be unable to think or concentrate, or you may be tormented by guilt. You may have your own recurring thoughts of death or suicide. "Why bother?" "What's the use?" "Why go on?" Depression is a natural response to tragic loss. As you go through the pain of your grief, it's very important that you discuss any signs of depression with your health care provider and/or a therapist.

▸ Acceptance: You begin to come to terms with the impermanence of life, your own mortality, and that of your loved ones. There may be fleeting moments of acceptance, or longer stretches when you experience some emotional stability, objectivity, and a broader perspective. "It's going to be okay." "I can accept even this." "I will meet these feelings of loss with kindness and wise choices." "I'm prepared to face what comes."

INNER COMPASS

Grief has its own pace and resolution for each of us. Listen to your inner wisdom to find your bearings, then chart your course in a way that feels true to you. Discover your own timing and make wise choices based on your own unique grieving process. Be patient and compassionate with yourself, maintain your Inner and Outer Supportive Resources, and stay open to the caring offered by others. In time your loss and grief will lead to a larger perspective on your loved one's life and on your own. You can experience more inner calm, deepen connection with your loved ones, and more fully live your life with enjoyment, contentment, and well-being.

The place to be on your healing journey is right where you are, resting in this moment, this breath, this step that you are taking right now. From time to time, check your Tool Kit to make sure that you're creating the support you need to continue moving forward on your healing journey toward the life you want to live.

INSTRUCTIONS FOR MEDITATION: SITTING AND WALKING

Sitting Meditation

During your grief and healing journey, it can be very helpful to sit silently for a period of time each day. If you're not familiar with meditation, here are some simple suggestions.

Create a meaningful space for meditation. You might include some special objects such as a flower, sacred articles, a photo, remembrances of your loved one, or lighting a candle.

Sit comfortably on a cushion with legs crossed or on a chair with your feet resting on the ground. Place your hands comfortably on your lap or your thighs, and allow your eyes to rest softly open or closed.

Allow your spine to lengthen, your head to be relaxed and upright, and your heart area to be open. Relax your body and let your belly soften. Release your facial muscles and allow an inner smile to bloom.

Gently bring awareness to your breathing. Breathe in a way that's natural and comfortable for you. Let your awareness rest lightly on each breath, letting go and relaxing with each out-breath.

Allow any thoughts and feelings to arise and pass in a very relaxed and nonjudgmental way. As thoughts arise, you might silently acknowledge them as "thinking" and then let them go, returning your awareness again and again to your relaxed body and gentle out-breath. Allow your thoughts and feelings to drift by like floating clouds. Open your awareness to the silent stillness—just sitting . . . breathing . . . and relaxing your body and mind.

Walking Meditation

Practicing meditation while you're walking can bring you more peace and well-being. Walking meditation is a valuable companion

practice with sitting meditation, and some may find a "moving meditation" more comfortable. The goal of walking meditation is not to arrive at
a destination, but the walking itself. Here are some suggestions.

Walk in a slow and mindful way, either inside or out of doors. Take
relaxed and leisurely steps, and let worries and emotions fall away. With
every step, become aware of each foot naturally lifting, moving, and then
meeting the earth.

Let your awareness rest with your breathing and the physical sensations throughout your body as you move, and open your senses to what
you're seeing, hearing, smelling, tasting, and touching in the moment.

If your attention wanders into thoughts about the past or the future,
let the thoughts go, and gently return your attention to the sensations of
movement and of the touch of each foot as it peacefully makes contact
with the earth.

Allow an inner smile to arise as you walk.

With every step simply remain present . . . relaxed . . . aware.

You may also silently repeat the following phrases, suggested by Thich
Nhat Hanh, with each step . . . "*I have arrived . . . I am home . . . In the here
. . . In the now.*"

TONGLEN MEDITATION:
TAKING IN PAIN AND SENDING OUT RELIEF

Tonglen is a practice for connecting with pain—your own
and that which is all around you, everywhere you go. It's a method for
overcoming the fear of suffering and awakening the compassion that's
inherent in all of us.

To begin, sit comfortably with your spine long and your belly soft.
Close your eyes, gently relax your body, and place your awareness lightly
on your breath. For a few breaths, rest your mind in a state of openness
and stillness. As you are ready:

1) Bring into your awareness someone you care about who is hurting
   and whom you wish to help—someone who is in some physical or
   emotional pain in their life. Breathe in with the wish to take away
   all of their pain, suffering, and fear. Then as you breathe out, send

them ease, happiness, or whatever would relieve their suffering. Breathe in their pain so they can be well and have more space to open and heal. Breathe out, sending them relaxation or whatever you feel would bring them relief and well-being.

2) When your *own* pain arises—fear, resistance, anger, helplessness, stuckness—change the focus and begin to do Tonglen for yourself, for what you are feeling. Breathe in your own pain, with the wish to be relieved of this suffering. And breathe out, sending to yourself whatever brings ease, relaxation, openness, compassion, and relief.

3) And now, make the practice bigger. As you practice Tonglen for the person you care about or for yourself, breathe in for the millions of other people just like you who at this very moment are feeling exactly the same pain and misery. And breathe out, for all those people, whatever would bring relief to their suffering. Simply contact what you're feeling and breathe in, take it in for all of us—and send out relief to all of us. Breathe in the feeling completely, letting it touch you, with a willingness to feel the suffering of humanity. And breathe out, radiating out compassion, loving kindness, freshness, openness, anything that heals, relaxes, and that helps you and others to open to and enjoy life. Let yourself contact the suffering and the joy of our human condition and how universal this experience is.

As you practice, breathe in as if through every pore, letting it melt your heart open, knowing that there is nowhere for it to get stuck inside. And breathe out as if through every pore, sending out, radiating out your compassion in all directions. Rather than doing what's habitual—whatever is painful is pushed away and whatever is pleasurable is held on to— Tonglen reverses that habit. When it's painful, breathe it in, let it touch you, overcoming your fear of pain. When it's delightful, send it out, and share it with others—relaxation, happiness, and well-being.

Tonglen can be done for those who are living or no longer living, for strangers, for animals, for anyone who is experiencing pain, fear, or any form of suffering. It can be practiced as a formal meditation or as an everyday habit, right on the spot—breathe in and breathe out, feel fully when you see or feel physical or emotional pain, with the wish that all beings be happy and free of suffering.*

*Adapted from Pema Chödrön, *When Things Fall Apart: Heart Advice for Difficult Times* (Boston, MA: Shambhala Publications, 2000) and *The Places that Scare You: A Guide to Fearlessness in Difficult Times* (Boston, MA: Shambhala Publications, 2005).

Appendix 2

Creating Support

Marilynne Chöphel, MFT
(A printable version of the "Creating Support" is available at
www.unfinishedconversation.com)

> *I can feel very alone in this journey, but I don't have to take this
> journey in isolation. We are conditioned by our society and culture
> not to talk about our pain. But if we don't talk, if we don't create a
> language to express our feelings, healing will not take place. We will
> continue to store up and re-create the cycles of suffering.*
>
> *What is helpful and necessary in this process is a safe container
> such as a therapeutic environment or a community of like-minded
> people who can assist, help, support, and encourage each other in
> this process of waking up.*
>
> —Claude Anshin Thomas*

WHEN YOU LOSE a loved one to suicide, there is a natural need to share
your experience with others who truly understand and to have a place
where you can talk openly with those who will listen without judgment.
Having your grief and loss met with compassion and held in the safety
and comfort of those you trust is an important part of resolution and
healing. Throughout your grieving and healing process, look for ways to
create support with others:

> ▸ **Support with a Journey Buddy:** Your Buddy might be a friend
> or relative of your lost loved one, or someone you trust and feel
> is caring. It can be most helpful to join in support with someone

---

*Claude Anshin Thomas, *At Hell's Gate: A Soldier's Journey from War to Peace* (Boston, MA:
Shambhala Publications, 2004).

who is also a survivor and can fully comprehend the depth and uniqueness of grief from suicide loss.

▶ **Support Group:** Meeting in a group with other survivors can help you feel less isolated and alone, offer comfort and validation for your grieving process, and create the opportunity to learn from each other. Support groups may be facilitated by peer survivors or by a professional. Because a group is a forum for equal sharing, it is important to consider if you are ready to witness and support others who are also grieving. (For information on support groups in your area, see Resources for Creating Support at the end of this appendix.)

▶ **Support with a Therapist:** Working with a licensed therapist or grief counselor can help you move through your grieving process in a safe and supportive way, and help to bring healing to depression, anxiety, and bereavement complicated with prior losses or past trauma. (For information on therapists in your area, see Resources for Creating Support at the end of this appendix.)

▶ **Support with** *Unfinished Conversation*: Consider reading *Unfinished Conversation* with your Journey Buddy or gather together other survivors, using the exercises at the end of each chapter as a way to explore, learn, and support each other.

SUPPORTIVE GUIDELINES: USING *UNFINSHED CONVERSTION* WITH OTHERS

Consider the following to help make your time with each other supportive and healing:

▶ **Safe Environment:** Create a safe and comfortable place to talk, cry, remember, question, and explore. Protect each other's privacy and confidentiality by not disclosing to others anything that is shared unless you have permission. "No alcohol or drugs" is a good policy to support clear and honest sharing. Have group members refrain from talking among themselves about what others in the group have said.

- ▶ **Schedule:** Regular meetings, either weekly or at least once every two weeks, are most helpful for continuity in the healing process. Allow some time before and after the meeting for informal connection to get to know and support each other. For groups, one and a half to two hours is a good length of time, depending upon the number of people participating.

- ▶ **Time Agreements:** Make clear agreements about the time, place, and length of each meeting. Having a formal beginning and ending, on time, focuses attention and helps create a container of safety and mutual support. To ensure that each person has equal time to share, you might want to use a timer or in some other way keep track of time, such as a "time-keeper" quietly ringing a bell.

- ▶ **Opening:** Sitting comfortably facing each other, with groups sitting in a circle so everyone can see each other, is very helpful in creating a sense of equality and support. Begin with a few minutes of silence to let go of the day, relax, and connect inward in the present moment. It can be helpful in the silence to remember the intention to heal and to support others in healing. Consider having each light a candle in honor of his or her loved one.

- ▶ **Brief Check-In:** Allow 3–5 minutes for each person to talk about their grieving and healing process, and/or any special needs or concerns.

- ▶ **Your Journey to Healing Exercises:** For each meeting, decide which chapters and exercises each will have read and worked with. During the meeting, be sure each person has a chance to either talk about their experience with the process or read from their journal if they wish. If anyone wants to remain silent, it is also important to honor that.

- ▶ **Stay Mindful and Present:** Remember that the intention is to heal, not to re-traumatize. Pause occasionally during the meeting to invite each person to become aware of their inner experience in the present moment. Consider using some of the *"Returning to the present moment . . ."* practices at the end of the exercise pages.

Bringing awareness to your physical sensations in the here-and-now is helpful for staying grounded in the present and connected with each other. Remember that as the suffering of the past is met with compassionate connection in the present, the pain can transform and heal.

▸ Closing: At the end of each meeting, allow a few minutes for each person to express gratitude, final thoughts, and to reflect on the time together. What was the hardest part? What was most valuable? What did that person learn that will support their grieving and healing process? If the group has lit candles, each person might one at a time blow out their flame with a wish or intention for their loved one and themself. You might end with holding hands, hugs if this is comfortable, or bowing to each other to honor your time together.

GUIDELINES FOR SPEAKING AND LISTENING

▸ When you are speaking: Take your time. Remember to relax your body, soften your belly, and breathe. When painful emotions arise, if you begin to feel overwhelmed or shut down, talk about what you need. Take time to pause in silence, allowing for deeper reflection and self-care. If you need to take a break from speaking, start again when you feel ready.

> *The Four-Fold Way: Show up and choose to be present. Pay attention to what has heart and meaning. Speak your truth without blame or judgment. Be open to outcome, not attached to outcome.*
> —Angeles Arrien, PhD, anthropologist, author, and corporate consultant

▸ When you are listening: Be present and listen deeply. Respect each person's opinions and unique way of grieving without analyzing, interpreting, judging, agreeing, or disagreeing, and avoid offering suggestions or focusing on solutions. Simply witness and honor each person's experience with gratitude for their honesty and courage. When silence arises, give the person the space to reflect, feel, and explore more deeply. Remember to relax your body, soften your belly, and breathe, especially if you begin to feel overwhelmed. Thank the speaker when he or she is done sharing.

> *Listening is all about giving. It heals through the power of generosity. It's an openhanded gift that asks nothing in return. Listening asks that we become empty. Willing to receive without agendas or judgment. Good listening requires both attention directed toward the other person, and also toward our own inner life. We need to pay careful attention to our own sensations, feelings, and intuitions. This is what allows us to resonate with another person.*
>
> —Frank Osteseski, Founding Director
> The Metta Institute and Zen Hospice

RESOURCES FOR CREATING SUPPORT

Support Groups: See Appendix 4 "Resources for Survivors of Suicide" for websites of organizations with survivor's support groups in your area, and its subsection Resources for Creating Survivor Support Groups that offers guidance for creating and facilitating suicide bereavement support groups..

Therapists: See Appendix 1, "Tool Kit for Your Journey to Healing" for its subsection Fellow Travelers and Guides that lists respected organizations that can help you find a therapist in your area who is licensed and trained in working with traumatic loss.

Appendix 3

Clinical Theory Behind *Unfinished Conversation's* Healing Process

Marilynne Chöphel MFT

(A printable version of the "Clinical Theory" is available at www.unfinished converstion.com)

The aftermath

Unprocessed grief blocks us from living and loving fully. All loss requires grieving, and any death can be traumatic. However, losing a loved one to suicide is especially traumatizing, and the bereavement complex. It overwhelms the ability to cope, and threatens physical, mental, emotional, and spiritual well-being. When faced with such distressing circumstances, the body is hard-wired to draw upon the most effective survival strategies available at the time—fight, flight, freeze, submit/collapse, or attach. Long after the events have ended, the intense responses in the mind and body are still felt and easily retriggered: emotional and physical distress, over- or underactivation, reliving the experience, sleep disturbance, self-limiting beliefs, self-destructive behavior, interpersonal challenges, emotional flooding, withdrawing and shutting down, and more.

It's important to remember that the responses to loss are unique to each person, and all are quite normal reactions to an event as life altering as losing someone you love to suicide. Any unresolved grief or trauma from the past also compounds the complexity of the current loss. Distressing symptoms remain trapped in the mind and body, easily triggered by everyday reminders of the painful past—sometimes for months or years—unless resolved in some way. The traces of the trauma that remain in your nervous system and mind *can* be completed and released, freeing the pain and fostering a renewed relationship with your self, your lost loved one, and your life.

THERE IS A WAY THROUGH

You can't change what happened in the past, but you can transform the mind's and the body's responses to the past. Modern neuroscience tells us that the way we respond to any experience causes neurons to fire, linking together various parts of the brain. Repeated firings of the same responses strengthen the neural pathways. This means that the more often we act and respond in a particular way, the more likely we are to continue doing so. This is how habits develop, and it's true for both positive and negative behaviors. However, neuroscience has also revealed the inherent neuro-plasticity of the brain—the lifelong capacity to change existing connections in the nervous system and even completely rewire them.

One of the main ways to alter old ineffective patterns of response, and cultivate more desirable behaviors and patterns of thinking, is through a process of "pairing" experiences. By activating the memory networks of the old unwanted patterns, while focusing attention on a new more desirable experience, the neural pathways of the old patterns are actually diminished. The new pathway can override the old, in effect "rewiring" it.

The Journal Exercises in *Unfinished Conversation* invite new experiences so that the old pathways can be responded to in new, more adaptive ways. Through reflection, writing, and creating new experiences, you are able to do *now* what wasn't able to be done *then*. You can create safety, take the time to scan for new options, make empowered choices, respond in ways that weren't possible at the time, and elicit a feeling of more competence or even triumph. As you repeatedly incline your mind toward what you want to create now, old ineffective patterns begin to be extinguished and are replaced with wiser choices. You begin to build a greater capacity for well-being.

THE GOAL IS TO HEAL

The exercises in the book are intended to help you move through the stages of trauma recovery in progressive, achievable steps to release the traumatic traces of the past and create a more healthy present. You are guided to create safety and stability, affirm your emotions, release the traumatic activation, transform your relationship to the past, find greater perspective and meaning, honor the relationship with your lost loved one, create the conditions for personal and relational well-being, and begin to live the life you want to live.

Remember that the goal is to heal, not re-live or re-traumatize. To avert getting hijacked by unregulated emotions, stuck in avoidance, or over-whelmed by memories, you are encouraged to complete the exercises within your optimal "window of tolerance," choosing a level of explora-tion and pacing that enables you to maintain safety and stability as you relate with the past in different ways.

THE TOOLS OF TRANSFORMATION

The healing process of *Unfinished Conversation* invites you to cultivate three primary tools. The first tool is mindful observation—the quality of compassionate awareness that notices, without judgment, your moment-by-moment experience inside and around you, and helps you step back from overwhelming experience to study it. You can take the time to pause and bring curiosity to the thoughts, feelings, and body sensations that are arising in the here-and-now in response to recalling the past. This mindful attention activates the frontal lobes of the higher brain to develop internal awareness, regulate your emotions, and learn from your experience.

The second tool is dual-awareness—the capacity to relate to the past, in small manageable doses, as you remain aware and grounded in the safety and connection of the present. When you intentionally focus atten-tion in an exercise, you activate the parts of the brain that can access the painful memories. You can begin to notice and uncouple the traumatic activation from the past—the distressing thoughts, emotions, impulses, physical sensations, self-limiting beliefs, incomplete actions—so that more adaptive responses can be discovered, restored, and used in the present.

The third tool is compassionate connection. A feeling of disconnection from not just your loved one but also from those around you and from yourself is natural after such sudden and tragic loss. And the journey to healing after suicide can feel very lonely, with the unfortunate stigma by many about suicide or mental illness. The exercises invite deepening awareness and compassionate connection with yourself, as you continue the conversation with your lost loved one. And they encourage you to communicate your feelings and needs with others— trusted individuals, a support group, and/or a mental health professional. (See Resources for Creating Support below.) As you begin to bring more understanding and compassion to yourself and your loved one, and reach out for support and connection with others who truly understand and care, shame and alienation can decrease, and a greater capacity for self-acceptance and supportive interpersonal connection can grow.

As your relationship to the old memory or pattern of responses is reorganized, you begin to come to terms with the traumatic past that is now over, as you create a more resourced, connected, and healthy present—to live fully and well.

RESOURCES FOR CREATING SUPPORT

Creating Support: See Appendix 2, "Creating Support" for ways to use *Unfinished Conversation* and help make your time with others supportive and healing.

Support Groups: See Appendix 4, "Resources for Survivors of Suicide" for websites of organizations with survivor's support groups in your area, and its subsection Resources for Creating Survivor Support Groups that offers guidance for creating and facilitating suicide bereavement support groups.

Therapists: See Appendix 1, "Tool Kit for Your Journey to Healing" for Fellow Travelers and Guides that lists respected organizations that can help you find a therapist in your area who is licensed and trained in working with traumatic loss.

Appendix 4

Resources for Survivors of Suicide

(A printable version of "Resources for Survivors of Suicide" is available at www.unfinishedconversation.com)

General Survivor Resources
Resources for Military Survivors
Resources for Families and Children Survivors
Resources for Creating Survivor Support Groups

General Survivor Resources

Unfinished Conversation Website
www.unfinishedconversation.com
> Excerpts from *Unfinished Conversation* Handouts: Tool Kit for Your Journey to Healing, Creating Support, Clinical Theory Behind *Unfinished Conversation*'s Healing Process, Common Feelings, and other supportive self-care handouts
> Web Links for Survivors (links to Survivor Support Groups in your area, and other survivor on-line resources)
> Suicide Prevention Resources
> Readings to Support Your Journey
> Resources for Health Professionals

American Association of Suicidology
www.suicidology.org

Suicide survivor support group directory.
http://www.suicidology.org/suicide-support-group-directory
> Books for survivors:

Comprehensive list of books reviewed and recommended by AAS

SOS Handbook, a quick-reference booklet for suicide survivors, available in English and Spanish.

Warning signs and risk factors for suicide

Statistics and fact sheets

Resources for clinicians

Resources for clinicians who have lost a patient or family member

Resources for those who have attempted suicide and for their families

American Foundation for Suicide Prevention

www.afsp.org

Suicide survivor support group directory.

http://www/afsp.org/coping-with-suicide/find-support/find-a -support-group

Online Support Groups

Books for Survivors:

Practiceal Guides for Coping with a Suicide Loss

Survivor Stories

Helping Children

For Adolescents and Teenagers

For Men

For Clinicians

Poetry and Inspiration

Understanding Suicide and Mental Illness

Surviving a Suicide Loss: A Resource and Healing Guide

Surviving a Suicide Loss: A Financial Guide

Survivor Outreach, Survivor e-Network,

Find a Therapist

Survivor Outreach, Survivor e-Network

Clinician-Survivors

Suicide Attempt Survivors

Personal Stories

Events:

International Survivors of Suicide Day

Out of the Darkness Walks

Honor a Loved One

Education & Training
Support Group Facilitators Education & Training

Canadian Association for Suicide Prevention
www.suicideprevention.ca
Find a Crisis Centre
Events and Conferences
World Suicide Prevention Day
About Suicide: Risk Assessment; Resiliency Factors
Survivor Support
After a Suicide; A Toolkit for Schools
A Guide for Early Responders Supporting Survivors Bereaved by
Suicide
National StandBy Response Service

International Association for Suicide Prevention (IASP)
www.iasp.info/postvention.php
Resources in English, Estonian, Flemish, French, Japanese, Polish,
Serbian, Spanish
IASP Special Interest Group: Postvention (Suicide Bereavement)
How to Start a Survivors' Group (IASP/WHO publication)
Survivor Guides
National Survivor Organizations
European Directory of Suicide Survivor Services
International Listing of Suicide Survivor Services
Newsletter

National Organization for People of Color Against Suicide (NOPCAS)
www.nopcas.com
Prevention, intervention, and postvention support services to the
families and communities impacted adversely by the effects of vio-
lence, depression, and suicide.
About Suicide
Surviving
Bereavement Support Groups
Resources and Events

Interviews

Training and Speakers Bureau

Survivors of Suicide (SOS)

www.survivorsofsuicide.com

Understanding suicide

Beyond surviving

How to help survivors heal

Suicide—FAQ

SOS Poetry for the Heart

SOS memorials with photos

Resource links

RESOURCES FOR MILITARY SURVIVORS

Suicide Wall

www.suicidewall.com

Dedicated to memorializing veterans of Vietnam, Iraq, and Afghanistan who have taken their own lives.

Tragedy Assistance Program for Survivors (TAPS)

Caring for the families of the fallen

www.taps.org

800-959-TAPS (8277)

Tragedy assistance resource 24/7 for anyone who has suffered the loss of a military loved one, regardless of the relationship to the deceased or the circumstance of the death. Suicide loss chat each month and annual gathering for suicide survivors.

RESOURCES FOR FAMILIES AND CHILDREN SURVIVORS

Compassionate Friends

www.compassionatefriends.org

Grief support after the death of a child for parents, siblings, and grandparents.

Annual national conference for bereaved families.

Dougy Center
The National Center for Grieving Children & Families
www.dougy.org
> Support for children, teens, young adults, and their families grieving
a death.
> Peer support groups, education, and training.

Friends and Families of Suicide/Parents of Suicide
www.pos-ffos.com
> Support group and memorial space for parents, friends, and families
who have lost someone to suicide.

Reachout.com
www.reachout.com
A website for teens that deals with all kinds of mental health issues.
Teens can read stories and watch videos of peers who have been through
similar issues. The website is monitored by mental health professionals
24/7. Based in Australia.
> Fact sheets
> Stories—from other young people sharing their experience
> Feature Stories—issues facing young people
> Forums—chat to other young people
> Videos—storeis and interviews

RESOURCES FOR CREATING SURVIVOR SUPPORT GROUPS

American Foundation for Suicide Prevention (AFSP)
www.afsp.org
Guidance for creating and facilitating suicide bereavement support
groups for adults, teens and children. The training program is offered as
a two-day comprehensive workshop, or a self-study manual with a DVD,
that includes structuring the meeting, facilitating the process, and dealing with difficulties, as well as sample openings, ground rules, closings,
handouts, and more.
> Facilitating Suicide Bereavement Support Groups: A Self-Study

Manual: Workbook and Companion DVD, "Facilitating Suicide Bereavement Support Groups: Skill-Building and Special Challenges"

Facilitating Suicide Bereavement Support Groups: The Two-day Program: Comprehensive training using lecture, interactive discussion, and role-playing to prepare participants to run an effective support group

Facilitating Suicide Bereavement Support Groups for Children and Teens: Comprehensive training program using lecture, interactive discussion, and role-playing

Appendix 5

Resources for Suicide Prevention

(A printable version of "Resources for Prevention of Suicide" is available at www.unfinishedconversation.com)

National Suicide Prevention Lifeline
www.suicidepreventionlifeline.org
> 1-800-273-TALK (8255)
> A free, 24-hour hotline available to anyone in suicidal crisis, emotional distress, or for survivors who need someone to talk with who understands your circumstances. Your call will be connected to the nearest crisis center to you.

> Veterans, call 1-800-273-8255 and press 1 to be routed to the Veterans Suicide Prevention Hotline.

American Association of Suicidology
www.suicidology.org
> Suicide Prevention Resources
> Warning Signs, Risk Factors, Statistics
> Books about Suicide: Comprehensive list of books reviewed and
> recommended by AAS
> Training & Accreditation
> Annual Conference

American Foundation for Suicide Prevention
www.afsp.org
> Understanding Suicide
> Preventing Suicide
> Coping with Suicide—for survivors
> Research, Advocacy, and Public Policy

Events:
  Out of the Darkness Walks to Prevent Suicide
  International Survivors of Suicide Day

The Canadian Association for Suicide Prevention
www.suicideprevention.ca
  Find a Crisis Centre
  Events and Conferences
  World Suicide Prevention Day
  About Suicide: Risk Assessment; Resiliency Factors

DoD/VA Suicide Outreach
Department of Defense/Veterans Administration
www.suicideoutreach.org
  Outreach Center 24/7 and Chat Online 24/7
  Warning Signs and Self-assessments
  Resources for Veterans

International Association for Suicide Prevention (IASP)
www.iasp.info/postvention.php
  Resources in English, Estonian, Flemish, French, Japanese, Polish,
    Serbian, Spanish
  Dedicated to preventing suicidal behavior, to alleviate its effects, and
    to provide a forum for academics, mental health professionals, cri-
    sis workers, volunteers, and suicide survivors.

National Center for Post-Traumatic Stress Disorder (PTSD)
United States Department of Veterans Affairs Department of Defense
www.ptsd.va.gov
  PTSD resources for people who have experienced trauma or have
    PTSD, and those who work with them.
  Public Section: Veterans, the General Public, Family & Friends
  Professional Section: Researchers, Providers & Professional Helpers
  Veterans Resources And Services

The Trevor Project
The leading national organization providing crisis intervention and suicide prevention services to lesbian, gay, bisexual, transgender, and questioning youth.
www.thetrevorproject.org
   Suicide Prevention
   Resources for Educators and Parents
   Events
   Advocacy

Suicide Prevention Resource Center (SPRC)
www.sprc.org
The only federally supported resource center devoted to providing technical assistance, training, and materials for suicide prevention practitioners and other professionals serving people at risk for suicide.
   Assessing and Managing Suicide Risk
   Online Trainings
   Suicide Prevention in Juvenile Correctional Facilities
   Suicide Prevention among LGBT Youth: for Professionals Who
      Serve Youth

U.S. Department of Veterans Affairs
www.va.gov
   Suicide Prevention Resources:
   www.mentalhealth.va.gov/suicide_prevention/
   Veterans Crisis Line: 1-800-273-8255 (Press 1)

Appendix 6

Readings to Support Your Journey to Healing: For Survivors and for Professionals Who Support Them

(A printable version of "Readings to Support Your Journey to Healing" is available at www.unfinishedconversation.com)

Grieving and Healing from Suicide

Blair, Pamela and Brook Noel. 2008. *I Wasn't Ready to Say Goodbye: A Companion Workbook*. Naperville, IL: Sourcebooks.

Cobain, Beverly and Jean Larch. 2006. *Dying to Be Free: A Healing Guide for Families after a Suicide*. Center City, MN: Hazelden.

Heckler, Richard A. 1994. *Waking Up Alive: The Descent, the Suicide Attempt, and the Return to Life*. New York, NY: Ballantine Books.

Jamison, Kay Redfield. 1999. *Night Falls Fast: Understanding Suicide*. New York, NY: Random House.

Joiner, Thomas. 2010. *Myths About Suicide*. Cambridge, MA: Harvard University Press.

Joiner, Thomas. 2005. *Why People Die by Suicide*. Cambridge, MA: Harvard University Press.

Lukas, Christopher and Henry M. Seiden. 2007. *Silent Grief: Living in the Wake of Suicide*. Philadelphia, PA: Jessica Kingsley Publishers.

Myers, Michael F. and Carla Fine. 2006. *Touched by Suicide: Hope and Healing after Loss*. New York, NY: Gotham Books.

Ostaseski, Frank. 2003. *Being a Compassionate Companion*. 3-CD audio set. San Francisco, CA: Zen Hospice Project.

Rando, Therese A. 1988. *How To Go On Living When Someone You Love Dies*. Lexington, MA: Lexington Books.

Schwiebert, Pat and Chuck DeKlyen. 2006. *Tear Soup: A Recipe for Healing after Loss*. Portland, OR: Grief Watch.

Smolin, Ann and John Guinan. 1993. *Healing after the Suicide of a Loved One*. New York, NY: Simon & Shuster, Inc.

Sogyal Rinpoche. 1994. *The Tibetan Book of Living and Dying*. San Francisco, CA: HarperCollins.

Stillwater, Michael and Gary Remal Malkin. 2003. *Graceful Passages: A Companion for Living and Dying*. Book and 2-CD set. Novato, CA: New World Library.

Tatelbaum, Judy. 1980. *The Courage to Grieve: Creative Living, Recovery, and Growth through Grief*. New York, NY: Lippincott & Crowell, Publishers, Inc.

HELPING CHILDREN AND TEENS

Dougy Center Collection. 2001. *After a Suicide: A Workbook for Grieving Kids*. Portland, OR: Dougy Center.

Requarth, Margo. 2006. *After A Parent's Suicide: Helping Children Heal*. Sebastopol, CA: Healing Hearts Press.

Rubel, Barbara. *But I Didn't Say Goodbye: Helping Children and Families After a Suicide*. 2009. Kendall Park, NJ: Griefwork Center, Inc.

CREATING WELLBEING

Arrien, Angeles. 2007. *The Second Half of Life: Opening the Eight Gates of Wisdom*. Boulder, CO: Sounds True.

Baraz, James and Shoshana Alexander. 2010. *Awakening Joy: 10 Steps That Will Put You on the Road to Real Happiness*. New York, NY: Bantam Books.

Beckwith, Michael Bernard. 2008. *Spiritual Liberation: Fulfilling Your Soul's Potential*. New York, NY: Atria Books.

Brach, Tara. 2004. *Radical Acceptance: Embracing Your Life with the Heart of a Buddha*. New York: Bantam.

Brach, Tara. 2012. *True Refuge: Finding Peace and Freedom in Your Own Awakened Heart*. New York: Random House Publishing Group.

Bridges, William. 2004. *Transitions: Making Sense of Life's Changes*. New York, NY: Da Capo Press.

Chödrön, Pema. 2007. *How to Meditate: A Practical Guide to Making Friends with Your Mind.* CD audio set. Boulder, CO: Sounds True, Inc.

Chödrön, Pema. 2010. *The Places That Scare You: A Guide to Fearlessness in Difficult Times.* Boston, MA: Shambala.

Chödrön, Pema. 2006. *Practicing Peace in Times of War.* Boston, MA: Shambhala.

Chödrön, Pema. 1997. *When Things Fall Apart: Heart Advice for Difficult Times.* Boston, MA: Shambhala Publications.

Dalai Lama, His Holiness the. 1998. *The Art of Happiness: A Handbook for Living.* New York, NY: Penguin Group.

Foster, Rick, and Greg Hicks. 1999. *How We Choose to Be Happy: The 9 Choices of Extremely Happy People—Their Secrets, Their Stories.* New York, NY: G. P. Putnam's Sons.

Germer, Christopher K. 2009. *The Mindful Path to Self-Compassion: Freeing Yourself from Destructive Thoughts and Emotions.* New York, NY: The Guilford Press.

Graham, Linda. 2013. *Bouncing Back: Rewiring Your Brain for Maximum Resilience and Well-Being.* Novato, CA: New World Library.

Hanson, Rick. 2009. *Buddha's Brain: The Practical Neuroscience of Happiness, Love, and Wisdom.* Oakland, CA: New Harbinger Publications, Inc.

Johnson, Stephen J. 2013. *The Sacred Path—The Way of the Spiritual Warrior: Journey to Mindful Manhood.* Woodland Hills, CA: Sacred Path Press.

Kabat-Zinn, Jon. 2009. *Full Catastrophe Living: Using the Wisdom of Your Body and Mind to Face Stress Pain, and Illness.* New York, NY: Delta Trade Paperbacks.

Kabat-Zinn, Jon. 2012. *Mindfulness for Beginners: Reclaiming the Present Moment—and Your Life.* Boulder, CO: Sounds True, Inc.

Kabat-Zinn, Jon. 1994. *Wherever You Go, There You Are.* New York, NY: Hyperion Books.

Kornfield, Jack. 2011. *A Lamp in the Darkness: Illuminating the Path Through Difficult Times.* Boulder, CO: Sounds True.

Luskin, Fred. 2009. *Forgive for Love: The Missing Ingredient for a Healthy and Lasting Relationship.* New York, NY: HarperCollins.

Meade, Michael. 2010. *Fate and Destiny: The Two Agreements of the Soul.* Seattle, WA: GreenFire Press.

Nhat Hanh, Thich. 1987. *The Miracle of Mindfulness: An Introduction to the Practice of Meditation.* Boston, MA: Beacon Press.

Nhat Hanh, Thich. 2011. *Reconciliation: Healing the Inner Child.* Berkeley, CA: Parallax Press.

Nhat Hanh, Thich. 2010. *Understanding Our Mind.* Berkeley, CA: Parallax Press.

Richmond, Lewis. 2012. *Aging as a Spiritual Practice: A Contemplative Guide to Growing Older and Wiser.* New York, NY: Penguin Group.

Siegel, Daniel J. 2007. *The Mindful Brain: Reflection and Attunement in the Cultivation of Well-Being.* New York, NY: Norton & Company, Inc.

Somé, Malidoma Patrice. 1999. *The Healing Wisdom of Africa: Finding Life Purpose through Nature, Ritual, and Community.* New York, NY: The Penguin Putnam, Inc.

HEALING FROM TRAUMA

Collins, Judy. 2007. *The Seven T's: Finding Hope and Healing in the Wake of Tragedy.* New York, NY: Penguin Group.

Cori, Jasmin Lee. 2007. *Healing from Trauma: A Survivor's Guide to Understanding Your Symptoms and Reclaiming Your Life.* Cambridge, MA: Marlowe & Company.

Johnson, Susan. 2002. *Emotionally Focused Couple Therapy with Trauma Survivors: Strengthening Attachment Bonds.* New York, NY: Guilford Publications, Inc.

Levine, Peter. 2005. *Healing Trauma: A Pioneering Program for Restoring the Wisdom of Your Body.* Book and CD set. Boulder, CO: Sounds True, Inc.

Levine, Peter A. and Gabor Mate. 2010. *In an Unspoken Voice: How the Body Releases Trauma and Restores Goodness.* Berkeley, CA: North Atlantic Books.

Ogden, Pat, Kekuni Minton, and Clare Pain. 2006. *Trauma and the Body: A Sensorimotor Approach to Psychotherapy.* New York, NY: W. W. Norton & Company.

Parnell, Laurel. 1997. *Transforming Trauma: EMDR—The Revolutionary New Therapy for Freeing the Mind, Clearing the Body, and Opening the Heart.* New York, NY: W. W. Norton & Company.

Schupp, Linda. 2004. *Assessing and Treating Trauma and PTSD*. Eau Claire, WI: Pesi Healthcare, LLC.

Shapiro, Francine. 2012. *Getting Past Your Past: Take Control of Your Life with Self- Help Techniques from EMDR Therapy*. Emmaus, PA: Rodale Books.

Siegel, Daniel J. and Marion Solomon. 2003. *Healing Trauma: Attachment, Mind, Body and Brain*. New York, NY: W. W. Norton & Company, Inc.

Thomas, Claude Anshin. 2006. *At Hell's Gate: A Soldier's Journey from War to Peace*. Boston, MA: Shambhala Publications.

Williams, Mary Beth and Soili Poijula. 2002. *The PTSD Workbook: Simple, Effective Techniques for Overcoming Traumatic Stress Symptoms*. Oakland, CA: New Harbinger Publications.

An extensive list of books for healing from suicide loss is available through the following organizations that screen, review, and summarize the books listed:

American Association of Suicidology

www.suicidology.org

American Foundation for Suicide Prevention

www.afsp.org

About the Authors

Robert Emile Lesoine, MA, Ed., is an educator, musician, writer, singer, and composer. His poetry, stories, and articles have been published in a number of alternative journals. He brings the strength and compassion developed through years of teaching music to inner-city children and teens to his support for survivors of suicide. Meditation and the study of Buddhism have been the ground of his daily life since 1990, and they lend a deep spiritual base to the healing process he offers in *Unfinished Conversation*. His own experience of healing his grief through writing is the basis of this book and his support of other survivors. Robert's website, www.unfinishedconversation.com, offers many resources for those healing from suicide and loss. He is the father of an adult son, Charlie, and lives in Santa Monica, California, with his wife Amy and their new dog Frisbee.

Marilynne Chöphel, MA, is a Licensed Marriage and Family Therapist who has offered depth psychotherapy since 1990 and specializes in the treatment of trauma. She brings to her work a strong foundation in mindfulness meditation and yoga, both of which she has taught for more than twenty-five years. The healing process of this book is inspired by her study of leading clinical treatments for trauma, as well as early experience working on a suicide crisis line, and as a therapist supporting individuals at the edge of life and death. Marilynne's website, www.dharmaspirit.com, offers resources and practical tools for those seeking healing through the challenges and losses in life. She is the mother of her adult sons, Brian and Kevin, two of her main teachers and companions on life's journey. She lives close to nature in San Rafael, California.

RELATED TITLES FROM PARALLAX PRESS

Awakening Joy, James Baraz and Shoshana Alexander

Being Peace, Thich Nhat Hanh

Beyond the Self, Thich Nhat Hanh

Cultivating the Mind of Love, Thich Nhat Hanh

Deep Relaxation, Sister Chan Khong

Happiness, Thich Nhat Hanh

Healing, Sister Dang Nghiem

Journeying East, Victoria Dimidjian

Learning True Love, Sister Chan Khong

The Long Road Turns to Joy, Thich Nhat Hanh

Love's Garden, Peggy Rowe-Ward and Larry Ward

A Mindful Way, Jeanie Seward Magee

Not Quite Nirvana, Rachel Neumann

Reconciliation, Thich Nhat Hanh

Solid Ground, Sylvia Boorstein, Norman Fisher,
and Tsoknyi Rinpoche

Parallax Press publishes books on the practice of mindfulness and daily life. As a non-profit publisher, we are committed to making these teachings accessible to everyone and preserving them for future generations. We believe that, in doing so, we help alleviate suffering and create a more peaceful world. For a copy of the catalog, please contact:

Parallax Press
P.O. Box 7355
Berkeley, CA 94707
Tel: (510) 525-0101
www.parallax.org

Monastics and laypeople practice the art of mindful living in the tradition of Thich Nhat Hanh at retreat communities worldwide. To reach any of these communities, or for information about individuals and families joining for a practice period, please contact:

Plum Village
13 Martineau
33580 Dieulivol, France
www.plumvillage.org

Magnolia Grove Monastery
123 Towles Rd.
Batesville, MS 38606
www.magnoliagrovemonastery.org

Blue Cliff Monastery
3 Mindfulness Road
Pine Bush, NY 12566
www.bluecliffmonastery.org

Deer Park Monastery
2499 Melru Lane
Escondido, CA 92026
www.deerparkmonastery.org

The Mindfulness Bell, a journal of the art of mindful living in the tradition of Thich Nhat Hanh, is published three times a year by Plum Village. To subscribe or to see the worldwide directory of Sanghas, visit www.mindfulnessbell.org

More Praise for *Unfinished Conversation*

"Suicide strikes our hearts unlike any other loss, often leaving us feeling a unique incompleteness. *Unfinished Conversation* guides the reader through a structured journaling process that may help on the path from tragedy to transformation. The authors have combined their own learning with classical grief work to provide a very accessible tool kit to support healing."

—Frank Ostaseski, Founder, The Metta Institute and The Zen Hospice Project, author of *Being a Compassionate Companion*

"A gentle, clinically grounded, and prayerful process of self-reflection that leads to a promise of perspective. It can be for the survivor, as well as for the fellow traveler and professional guide. Through its wisdom and wealth of tools of transformation, it's an invaluable gift, a fitting self-conversation partner on the road to healing and new life."

—David A. Lichter, DMin, Executive Director, National Association of Catholic Chaplains

"A highly recommended book for people navigating the aftermath of suicide in search of meaning, healing, and freedom. It can be immensely useful for individuals who have lost loved ones by suicide, and those of us who accompany them—their family, friends, support group members, and counselors. The book is filled with many practical suggestions and universal understandings that are adoptable to one's particular spirituality and situation. A book about freedom and the spirit of *L'Chaim*—To Life."

—Chaplain Bruce Feldstein MD, Founder and Director of The Jewish Chaplaincy, Stanford University Medical Center

"A much-needed tool and source of hope for the family and friends of those who commit suicide, a valuable resource that addresses each of the challenges and each stage of grieving in a very moving, mindful way."
—Janina Fisher PhD, Assistant Director, Sensorimotor Psychotherapy Institute, and leader in the treatment of trauma

"Suicide (and other traumatic events) shatters the soul of the survivor. This warm, wise, and loving book will open many a door for people who have experienced significant loss and long for deep healing to restore their feeling of wholeness. Thank you for a beautiful and understanding work."
—Bryan Wittine, PhD, Jungian Psychoanalyst

"A roadmap from tragedy, through recovery, to eventual healing. It compassionately tackles a tough topic in a user-friendly, highly readable way. The authors have answered the call to address one of the biggest challenges facing our society today."
—Stephen J. Johnson, PhD, MFT, Executive Director, The Men's Center Los Angeles, author of *The Sacred Path*

"The emotional storm felt by family members after suicide, bewildering and profound, must be worked with over time until gradually a sense of acceptance occurs. The authors have given us a wonderful and poignant portrayal of this process along with a map that all of us can follow when we need one, whether dealing with suicide or some other personal loss, be it our own or helping someone else."
—Gill Cryer MD, PhD, Director, Trauma/Emergency Surgery and Critical Care Program, UCLA Medical Center

"This creative intervention takes us on a journey of healing that is practical, accessible, and offers an abundance of compassion and wisdom for survivors and professionals, as well as students of the healing arts. The healing potential offered here is priceless!"
—Dean Chambers LCSW, Special Crisis Response Coordinator, Critical Care Manager, Alameda County Behavioral Health Care Services

"Just what we survivors need: a safe, enlightening, guided path into and through our fear and grief."

—Beverly Cobain RN, author of *When Nothing Matters Anymore* and co-author of *Dying to Be Free*. Her cousin, Kurt Cobain, lead singer of the band Nirvana, died from suicide in 1994.

"A compelling account of one man's personal journey depicting the human capacity to search and find meaning, love, and beauty in both life and death . . . even in the midst of great sorrow."

—Jean Larch, co-author of *Dying To be Free*

"This book has the potential of informing prisoners considering suicide of the immense suffering of those they leave behind, and perhaps that can help to give them the courage to continue on—I hope so."

—Sita Lozoff, co-founder, The Prison-Ashram Project and the Human Kindness Foundation

"A tremendous resource for those who are struggling to make sense of something that just doesn't make sense. It explains the inexplicable, and brings comfort to those who are grieving, while allowing them to begin their own journey of grief and healing."

—BJ Ayers, Executive Director and Founder, Grace for 2 Brothers Foundation

"Every year over 200,000 Americans suddenly, unwillingly, become the survivors of the suicide of someone they love. Their experience of grief is completely different and vastly more painful than for those people who grieve for other deaths. A helpful guide for what to expect at various stages and a set of strategies for handling these phenomena is a real gift for each of these people."

—Eve R. Meyer, Executive Director, San Francisco Suicide Prevention